The Cost
of Living

The Cost of Living

A Working Autobiography

Deborah Levy

BLOOMSBURY PUBLISHING
NEW YORK • LONDON • OXFORD • NEW DELHI • SYDNEY

BLOOMSBURY PUBLISHING
Bloomsbury Publishing Inc.
1385 Broadway, New York, NY 10018, USA

BLOOMSBURY, BLOOMSBURY PUBLISHING, and the Diana logo
are trademarks of Bloomsbury Publishing Plc

First published in 2018 in Great Britain by Hamish Hamilton
This edition published in the United States 2018

The line on page 72 is taken from "April Rain Song" in *The Collected Poems
of Langston Hughes* copyright © Langston Hughes, 1994, reproduced
by kind permission of David Higham and Harold Ober Associates.

Deborah Levy has quoted from her essay on Fashion and Freedom,
co-commissioned by Manchester Literary Festival 2016,
Manchester Art Gallery, and 14–18 NOW.

Bloomsbury Publishing Plc does not have any control over, or responsibility for, any
third-party websites referred to or in this book. All Internet addresses given in this
book were correct at the time of going to press. The author and publisher regret
any inconvenience caused if addresses have changed or sites have ceased
to exist, but can accept no responsibility for any such changes.

ISBN: HB: 978-1-63557-191-2; eBook: 978-1-63557-192-9

LIBRARY OF CONGRESS CATALOGING-IN-PUBLICATION DATA IS AVAILABLE.

2 4 6 8 10 9 7 5 3 1

Typeset by Westchester Publishing Services
Printed and bound in the U.S.A. by Berryville Graphics Inc., Berryville, Virginia

To find out more about our authors and books visit www.bloomsbury.com
and sign up for our newsletters.

Bloomsbury books may be purchased for business or promotional use.
For information on bulk purchases please contact Macmillan Corporate
and Premium Sales Department at specialmarkets@macmillan.com.

You're always more unreal to yourself than other people are.

           – Marguerite Duras, *Practicalities* (1990)

CONTENTS

ONE

THE BIG SILVER

As Orson Welles told us, if we want a happy ending, it depends on where we stop the story. One January night I was eating coconut rice and fish in a bar on Colombia's Caribbean coast. A tanned, tattooed American man sat at the table next to me. He was in his late forties, big muscled arms, his silver hair pinned into a bun. He was talking to a young English woman, perhaps nineteen years old, who had been sitting on her own reading a book, but after some ambivalence had taken up his invitation to join him. At first he did all the talking. After a while she interrupted him.

Her conversation was interesting, intense and strange. She was telling him about scuba-diving in Mexico, how she had been underwater for twenty minutes and then surfaced to find there was a storm. The sea had become a whirlpool and she had been anxious about making it back to the boat. Although her story was about surfacing from a dive to discover the weather had changed, it was also about some sort of undisclosed hurt. She gave him a few clues about that (there was someone on the boat who she thought should have come to save her) and then she glanced at him to check if he knew that she was talking about the storm in a disguised way. He was not that interested and managed to move his knees in a way that jolted the table so that her book fell to the floor.

He said, 'You talk a lot don't you?'

She thought about this, her fingers combing out the ends of her hair while she watched two teenage boys selling cigars and football shirts to tourists in the cobbled square. It was not that easy to convey to him, a man much older than she was, that the world was her world too. He had taken a risk when he invited her to join him at his table. After all, she came with a whole life and libido of her own. It had not occurred to him that she might not consider herself to be the *minor character* and him the major character. In this sense, she had unsettled a boundary, collapsed a social hierarchy, broken with the usual rituals.

She asked him what it was that he was scooping up from his bowl with tortilla chips. He told her it was ceviche, raw fish marinated in lime juice, which was written in the menu in English as *sexvice* – 'It comes with a condom,' he said. When she smiled, I knew she was making a bid to be someone braver than she felt, someone who could travel freely on her own, read a book and sip a beer alone in a bar at night, someone who could risk an impossibly complicated conversation with a stranger. She took up his offer to taste his ceviche, then dodged his offer to join him for a night swim in an isolated part of the local beach, which, he assured her, was 'away from the rocks'.

After a while, he said, 'I don't like scuba-diving. If I had to go down deep, it would be for gold.'

'Oh,' she said. 'It's funny you say that. I was thinking my name for you would be the Big Silver.'

'Why Big Silver?'

'It was the name of the diving boat.'

He shook his head, baffled, and moved his gaze from her breasts to the neon sign for Exit on the door. She smiled again, but she didn't mean it. I think she knew she had to calm the turbulence she had brought with her from Mexico to Colombia. She decided to take back her words.

'No, Big Silver because of your hair and the stud above your eyebrow.'

'I'm just a drifter,' he said. 'I drift about.'

She paid her bill and asked him to pick up the book he had jolted to the floor, which meant he had to bend down and reach under the table, dragging it towards him with his foot. It took a while, and when he surfaced with the book in his hand, she was neither grateful nor discourteous. She just said, 'Thanks.'

While the waitress collected plates heaped with crab claws and fish bones, I was reminded of the Oscar Wilde quote 'Be yourself; everyone else is already taken.' That was not quite true for her. She had to make a bid for a self that possessed freedoms the Big Silver took for granted – after all he had no trouble being himself.

You talk a lot don't you?

To speak our life as we feel it is a freedom we mostly choose not to take, but it seemed to me that the words she wanted to say were lively inside her, mysterious to herself as much as anyone else.

Later, when I was writing on my hotel balcony, I thought about how she had invited the drifting Big Silver to read between the lines of her undisclosed hurt. She could have stopped the story by describing the wonder of all she had seen in the deep calm sea before the storm. That would have been a happy ending, but she did not stop there. She was asking him (and herself) a question: Do you think I was abandoned by that person on the boat? The Big Silver was the wrong reader for her story, but I thought on balance that she might be the right reader for mine.

Two

THE TEMPEST

Everything was calm. The sun was shining. I was swimming in the deep. And then, when I surfaced twenty years later, I discovered there was a storm, a whirlpool, a blasting gale lifting the waves over my head. At first I wasn't sure I'd make it back to the boat and then I realized I didn't want to make it back to the boat. Chaos is supposed to be what we most fear but I have come to believe it might be what we most want. If we don't believe in the future we are planning, the house we are mortgaged to, the person who sleeps by our side, it is possible that a tempest (long lurking in the clouds) might bring us closer to how we want to be in the world.

Life falls apart. We try to get a grip and hold it together. And then we realize we don't want to hold it together.

When I was around fifty and my life was supposed to be slowing down, becoming more stable and predictable, life became faster, unstable, unpredictable. My marriage was the boat and I knew that if I swam back to it, I would drown. It is also the ghost that will always haunt my life. I will never stop grieving for my long-held wish for enduring love that does not reduce its major players to something less than they are. I am not sure I have often witnessed love that achieves all of these things, so perhaps this ideal is fated to be a phantom. What sort of questions does this phantom ask of me? It asks political questions for sure, but it is not a politician.

When I was travelling in Brazil, I saw a brightly coloured caterpillar as thick as my thumb. It looked as if it had been designed by Mondrian, its body marked with symmetrical squares of blue, red and yellow. I couldn't believe my eyes. Most peculiar of all, it appeared to have two vibrant red heads, one on either end of its body. I stared at it over and over again to check if this could possibly be true. Perhaps the sun had gone to *my* head, or I was hallucinating from the smoky black tea that I sipped every day while I watched children play soccer in the square. It was possible, as I discovered later, that the caterpillar presented a false head to protect itself from predators. At this time, I could not decide which part of the bed I wished to sleep on. Let's say the pillow on my bed faced south; sometimes I slept there and then I changed the pillow so it faced north and slept there too. In the end I placed a pillow on each end of the bed. Perhaps this was a physical expression of being a divided self, of not thinking straight, of being in two minds about something.

When love starts to crack the night comes in. It goes on and on. It is full of angry thoughts and accusations. These tormenting internal monologues don't stop when the sun rises. This is what I resented most, that my mind had been abducted and was full of Him. It was nothing less than an occupation. My own unhappiness was starting to become a habit, in the way that Beckett described sorrow becoming 'a thing you can keep adding to all your life . . . like a stamp or an egg collection'.

When I returned to London, my local Turkish newsagent gave me a fur pom-pom key ring. I wasn't sure what to do with it, so I attached it to my handbag. There is something very uplifting about a pom-pom. I went for a walk in Hyde Park with a male colleague and it bounced around in a light-hearted manner as we kicked our way through the autumn leaves. It was a free spirit, madly joyful, part animal, part something else. It was so much happier than I was. He wore a delicate ring with a tiny sleepy diamond embedded in the latticed gold band. He said, 'My wife chose this wedding ring for me. It's Victorian, not really my style, but it reminds me of her.' And then he said, 'My wife crashed the car again.' Ah, I thought, as we walked past the golden trees, *she does not have a name. She is a wife.* I wondered why my male colleague often forgot the names of most of the women he met at social events. He would always refer to them as someone's wife or girlfriend, as if that was all I needed to know.

If we don't have names, who are we?

I cried like a woman when I knew my marriage was over. I have seen a man cry like a woman but I'm not sure I have seen a woman cry like a man. The man who cried like a woman was at a funeral and he did not so much cry as wail, sob and weep; his tears were very strong. His shoulders were shaking, his face was blotchy, he reached into his jacket pocket and took out tissues to press against his eyes. Every one of them fell apart. Strange sounds and utterances came from his diaphragm. It was a very expressed grief.

I thought he was weeping for all of us in that moment. Everyone else was crying in a more socially conscious way. When I spoke to him at the wake afterwards, he told me that this bereavement had made him aware that in his own life, 'Love had signed its name in the visitors' book but never moved in.'

He wondered what had stopped him from being bolder. We were sipping fine Irish whiskey, a brand favoured by the exceptional man who had died. I asked him if he and this man had been lovers? He said yes, on and off for many years, but they had never risked making themselves vulnerable to each other. They had never owned up to their love. When he asked me why my marriage was shipwrecked, his own honesty made it possible to speak more freely. After I had spoken for a while, he said, 'It seems to me that you would be better off finding another way to live.'

I imagined the conversation that I had never had with the father of my children being found one day in the black box that was flung to the bottom of the ocean when the boat crashed. One rainy Tuesday in the far future, it would be found by artificial life who would gather round to listen to the sad, strong voices of human beings in pain.

The best thing I ever did was not swim back to the boat. But where was I to go?

THREE

NETS

We sold the family house. This action of dismantling and packing up a long life lived together seemed to flip time into a weird shape; a flashback to leaving South Africa, the country of my birth, when I was nine years old and a flash-forward to an unknown life I was yet to live at fifty. I was unmaking the home that I'd spent much of my life's energy creating.

To strip the wallpaper off the fairy tale of The Family House in which the comfort and happiness of men and children have been the priority is to find behind it an unthanked, unloved, neglected, exhausted woman. It requires skill, time, dedication and empathy to create a home that everyone enjoys and that functions well. Above all else, it is an act of immense generosity to be the architect of everyone else's well-being.

This task is still mostly perceived as women's work. Consequently, there are all kinds of words used to belittle this huge endeavour. If the wife and mother has been impregnated by society, she is playing everyone's wife and mother. She has built the story the old patriarchy has designed for the nuclear heterosexual family, and of course added a few contemporary flourishes of her own. To not feel at home in her family home is the beginning of the bigger story of society and its female discontents. If she is not too defeated by the societal story she has enacted with hope, pride, happiness, ambivalence and rage, she will change the story.

To unmake a family home is like breaking a clock. So much time has passed through all the dimensions of that home. Apparently, a fox can hear a clock ticking from forty yards away. There was a clock on the kitchen wall of our family home, less than forty yards from the garden. The foxes must have heard it ticking for over a decade. It was now all packed up, lying face down in a box.

My kind neighbour saw me standing in the garden as the doors of the removal van slammed and the driver started the engine. She asked if I needed to rest. I lay down for an hour on her sofa. As I was about to leave, she asked, 'What are those things there?' She was pointing to my daughters' childhood fishing nets, which I hadn't packed with everything else. One was yellow, the other blue, still coated with grains of sand. They had used these nets to catch small fish on seaside holidays, wading up to their knees in the sea, waiting for something incredible to come their way. The nets, five foot long, were now leaning dreamily against my neighbour's Victorian bay window.

Their father and I agreed that we would live separately but we would always live together in the lives of our children. There are only loving and unloving homes. It is the patriarchal story that has been broken. All the same, most children who grow up in that story will struggle, along with everyone else, to compose another one.

FOUR

LIVING IN YELLOW

Night after night, I went around recognizing myself in an idea
that suggested general disintegration and, at the same time,
new composition.
— Elena Ferrante, *The Story of the Lost Child* (2015)

That November I moved with my daughters to a flat on the
sixth floor of a large shabby apartment block on the top of a
hill in North London. Apparently a *restoration programme*
was due to start in this apartment block, but it never seemed
to start. The floors of the communal corridors were covered
in grey industrial plastic for three years after we moved in.
The impossibility of repairing and rehabilitating a vast old
building seemed gloomily appropriate at this time of disintegration and rupture. The process of restoration, the bringing
back and repairing of something that existed before, in this

case an art deco building that was falling apart, was the wrong metaphor for this time in my life.

I did not wish to restore the past. What I needed was an entirely new composition.

It was a bitter winter. The communal heating system had broken down. The heating was off, the hot water was off, and sometimes the cold water was off too. I had three halogen heaters on the go and twelve large bottles of mineral water stored under the sink. When the water was switched off, the toilet would not flush. Someone had anonymously written a note and stuck it on the lift door. *HELP. Please help. The flats are unbearably cold, could someone DO something.* My oldest daughter, who had begun her first year at university, joked that student life was a luxury in comparison. For a few weeks after she departed to begin her degree, I woke up in the small hours with a queasy feeling that something was wrong. Where was my oldest child? And then I remembered, and I knew that we were all of us moving forwards into another kind of life.

It was futile to try to fit an old life into a new life. The old fridge was too big for the new kitchen, the sofa too big for the lounge, the beds the wrong shape to fit the bedrooms. Most of my books were in boxes in the garage with the rest of the family house. More urgently, I no longer had a study at the most professionally busy time in my life. I wrote wherever I could and concentrated on making a home for my daughters. I could say that it was these years that were the most self-sacrificing, and not the years in our nuclear-family unit. Yet, to be making this kind of home, a space for a mother and her daughters, was so hard and humbling, profound and interesting, that to my surprise I found I could work very well in the chaos of this time.

I was thinking clearly, lucidly; the move up the hill and the new situation had freed something that had been trapped and stifled. I became physically strong at fifty, just as my bones were supposed to be losing their strength. I had energy because I had no choice but to have energy. I had to write to support my children and I had to do all the heavy lifting. Freedom is never free. Anyone who has struggled to be free knows how much it costs.

I heaved two huge stone plant pots from the garden of the family house and placed them on the balcony outside my bedroom. This balcony was the size of a long, thin kitchen table. There was just about room for a tiny, round garden table and two chairs. The pots resembled ocean liners docking in a tiny pond. They did not belong here. Not in this new life living in the sky with long views over London. The bleak communal corridor walls of the building had been painted a speckled grey in the 1970s, which I suppose matched the grey plastic that had been laid over the mangy green carpets. These corridors were lit all day and all night, a sinister, unchanging twilight. At other times they felt amniotic and trippy, as if we were floating in grey membrane. My friends thought they looked like something out of *The Shining*.

I started to call them The Corridors of Love.

Anyone making a delivery to the flat for the first time (there were over a hundred flats) looked slightly panicked and disorientated when I opened the front door. If we squeezed our eyes half shut we could pretend the corridors were a version of Don Draper's Manhattan residence in *Mad Men* – after a minor catastrophe had occurred. Perhaps not an earthquake, but an earth tremor, in which the new inhabitants of the building could glimpse what it used to be like in the old days. Yet, once we were inside the flat itself, it was light and airy after our dark Victorian family house. We were living with the sky from dawn to dusk, its silver mists and moving clouds and shape-shifting moons.

Sometimes at night the faraway stars seemed very close when I wrote on the tiny balcony, wrapped in a coat. I had swapped the book-lined study of my former life for a starry winter night sky. It was the first time I enjoyed a British winter.

I had been given two small flowering strawberry trees and they liked living on the balcony. How did this evergreen plant manage to produce scarlet berries in November? Apparently it was a plant that had evolved before the last Ice Age, so maybe it liked the cold. Some nights I wrote in my bedroom like a student, but without the beer, spliffs and crisps. In my old life, I used to write early in the morning, but now I had become a morning and a night person. I'm not sure what happened to sleep in this phase. After all the heavy lifting, it was a shock to be figuring out how to land the cadence of one single sentence. Three days after the move, in the early hours towards dawn, a giant sleepy bee landed on my computer screen. At the same time, I could hear buzzing around the bulb in my lamp. When I looked up, there were five bees in my room, more energetic than the plump czarina dozing on my screen. I have always had encounters with bees in my life and often wondered why the main protagonists in fairy tales set in woods and forests are rarely bitten and stung by insects. When Little Red Riding Hood made her way through the spruce and beech trees of the woods to deliver bread to her grandmother, her shins would have been devoured by mosquitoes long before the wolf threatened to eat her up. And what about the ants, spiders, ticks and horseflies with which she and we share our living? Where had these London winter bees come from? Perhaps they had flown in after visiting the strawberry trees. It seemed like a good omen that the bees were happy to live with me in my happiness and misery. How was I to live with them? I switched off the lamp, then my laptop and left the room. As I stretched out on the sofa in the living room, twelve unpacked boxes still stacked against the walls, an Emily Dickinson poem came to mind. I could say it flew into my mind from nowhere, but there is no such thing as nowhere. All my Dickinson books were getting damp in the boxes of books mouldering in the garage. They had been on my mind.

> Fame is a bee.
> It has a song –
> It has a sting –
> Ah, too, it has a wing.

I wished that fame had given Emily Dickinson a wing when she was alive. I knew what it felt like to be undermined, and how, as she told us, hope is the thing with feathers that never stops singing, despite discouragement and neglect. Emily Dickinson had become a recluse. Maybe she was punishing herself for her bid for freedom, her bid not to be mastered? Another of her poems came in from nowhere, which is always somewhere, and it had the word *wife* in it. I could only remember the first line:

I'm 'wife' – I've finished that –

I wondered what it was that she had finished, and then I fell asleep in my jeans and boots, like a cowgirl, except the sky was my prairie.

That winter, my daughter and I liked to eat oranges for breakfast. We peeled and sliced the fruit the night before, made a syrup from water and honey and chilled them in the fridge. We became more experimental, adding cardamom seeds and rose water, but decided it was like eating blossom too early in the morning. The bees would have liked it, but I did not want them to take over the joint. I had bought one of those clocks that have a different bird sing every hour. In the morning at seven the wren made its call to the real birds singing in the dark winter trees. At 4pm it was dark again when the great spotted woodpecker began to drill and drum. Returning home at night I could sometimes hear the nightingale as I walked through the grey Corridors of Love.

While my older daughter was at university, we had shrunk from a family of four to a family of two. It was hard to get used to the empty table and lack of shouting. So I borrowed another family I knew from down the road and invited them to lunch most Sundays. That made six of us, and our tiny family became a bigger, noisier affair. They were a clever family, this lot down the road. They knew that I wanted to extend my own family, but they never said that to me, in a hushed conspiratorial way. They arrived in a good mood or a bad mood, depending on who had lost their trainers or door key or phone. We got stuck into lunch, drank a lot of wine and they laughed at my bird clock. As they usually arrived at one o'clock they were serenaded by the chaffinch. By the time they left, the barn owl had begun its call.

When I wasn't writing and teaching and unpacking boxes, my attention was on mending the blocked pipes under the basin in the bathroom. This involved unscrewing all the parts, placing a bucket under the pipes and not knowing what to do next. I had borrowed a mysterious machine from the cardiologist who lived downstairs. It was like a Hoover except it had wires which were then inserted into the tube. It was early morning and I was wearing what is sometimes called a French postman's jacket over my nightdress. It was not a deliberate decision to wear a blue postman's jacket for a plumbing job, not at all, it just happened to be hanging on the hook in the bathroom and it kept me warm. The clash between the thick utilitarian cotton of the jacket and the flimsy nightdress seemed to sum everything up for me, but I was not sure what the final sum equalled. Now that I was no longer married to society, I was transitioning into something or someone else. What and who would that be? How could I describe this odd feeling of dissolving and recomposing? Words have to open the mind. When words close the mind, we can be sure that someone has been reduced to nothingness.

To amuse myself (there was no one else around) I began to think about the genre of the female nightdress in relation to plumbing. The one I was wearing was black silk and I suppose quite sensual in a generic way. I could promenade in it and I could masquerade in it, given that femininity was a masquerade anyway. I could see that black silk was a classic in the female nightwear genre. To add to the mix, I was also wearing what my daughters called my 'shaman slippers'. They were black suede ankle boots trimmed with abundant, queasily realistic fake furs, one of which hung like a small tail, whipping my ankles as I walked around the flat looking for a gadget called a Master Plunger. The slippers were a gift from my best male friend, who thought I needed some 'insulation', as he put it – which might be a plumbing term for covering up something that is exposed and raw. I appreciated the fur boots with their comforting warmth and magical properties (I suppose my phantasy was that I had skinned the animals myself) and the postman's jacket seemed to be a counterpoint to the black silk nightdress.

I was the man. I was the woman.

Perhaps I was the shaman?

That was a dimension I wished to explore further. The male shaman often wore female clothing. They had the top temple job. I had heard that in Korea, a female shaman is permitted to wear male clothing so as to receive a masculine presence into her body. Would that be my blue postman's jacket? The shaman has to journey to other worlds, just as I had to journey into the interior of the system under the basin to see how it was connected to the blocked pipes near the bath. My hands started to tingle, perhaps to give me strength for the DIY battles ahead. What came up through the pipes after much excavation with the help of the mysterious machine and the Master Plunger was a thick, slimy knot of human hair. Plumbing was like archaeology. The hair was a human artefact, dredged up from the depths. The Master Plunger was an object of beauty and function. When the water ran freely down the plughole again, I whirled the clump of hair in lonely victory. I began to think I could not only excavate ancient Rome, but plumb it too. I knew I would have to get a mysterious machine of my own. The cardiologist had invited me to join him for a glass of wine after I returned his tools. I might one day risk falling in love again, but I was not going to lose my heart to the cardiologist.

That same day I made a garden in the bathroom. I planted a tall cactus and other succulents and placed them on the shelf next to the bath. They were spiky, some of them covered in sharp white thorns. The steam from the hot water seemed to send them into an erotic frenzy because the succulents began to grow at an accelerated pace.

As everything in my new home became literally smaller (except for the succulents), my life became bigger. At this difficult time, I took every job offered to me and winced when the bills flew through the letterbox. I began to realize that what I needed was enough of the right things. The light and sky and balcony were the right things. My children finding their way through the new story, starting to shape it and make it their own and being in close contact with their father, all of these were right things. A flat full of singing teenagers when my youngest daughter brought her friends back after school was the right thing. Not having a calm place to write was the wrong thing. Not living with animals was the wrong thing. But how could we live with an animal in a flat on the sixth floor?

We talked about a goldfish but decided it was better off in a pond. My daughter said she would get a mouse, but it didn't happen. We talked about a parrot, but that didn't happen either. At one point she talked about capturing a squirrel from the park and bringing it home.

Did that happen? Did she groom its tail every morning before she went off to school? It was what she wanted, but it didn't happen. Instead she lay in bed and read *The Great Gatsby*, then told me that F. Scott Fitzgerald wasn't a very good writer. Sometimes an animal is more consoling than a book.

My friend Gemma said to me, 'You have to get your bedroom working for you. Build a desk. Build shelves. Bring up the boxes from the garage and unpack your books. Have a go at living with colour.' By this she meant painting the walls a colour that was not white. 'Yellow would be good for you,' she insisted. 'It clears up emotions and gives us a bigger sense of things.' When she said that, I remembered painting the bedroom ceiling in the family house with a colour called English Skylight. The ceiling looked like a dull leaden sky. Even when the sun was shining outside, it was raining inside. Every day and every night.

In my new life I was going to commit to living with colour.

I painted the walls in my bedroom yellow. I bought sumptuous orange silk curtains in a charity shop. I put up an African shield made from chicken feathers that had been dyed pink. It was two foot wide and looked like a large full-blown flower. The shield was stitched together in a way that allowed it to open and close. Yet nailed to the wall it was always open at a time when I was emotionally closed. I needed a shield to defend myself from the rage of my old life. I suppose I could say that I was now shielded by a flower.

A heroine of mine was the eighty-one-year-old South African artist Esther Mahlangu, who taught herself to become an artist at the age of ten by watching her mother and grandmother paint with chicken feathers. She herself was a work of art – the beading on her clothes, the bangles on her hands, neck and feet. I wanted to speak to her, but I did not know what I wanted to say.

Esther, I don't know how to live in yellow. I don't know how to live in my life.

The yellow walls were driving me mad. The orange silk curtains were like waking up to a rash.

I took down the shield and painted all but one wall white again. I replaced the shield with a framed screenprint of Oscar Wilde. Then I went off to tackle the moths in the kitchen. They were like something out of a García Márquez novel, flying around like tiny blind demons, satiated on the self-raising flour and oats that lured them to my cupboards.

The moths seemed to like landing on the two photographs I had stuck on to the fridge door with magnets. One was of the British sculptor Barbara Hepworth, age sixty, a carving tool in her hand, leaning into the giant sphere of wood she was shaping. She had burst solid form open to make a pierced form, a hole, after the birth of her first child in 1931. Hepworth described sculpture as 'the three-dimensional realization of an idea'.

The other photograph was of the sculptor Louise Bourgeois, age ninety, an iron carving tool in her hand, leaning over a white sculptural sphere that came to her waist. In the photograph she was wearing a chiffon blouse under a black tunic, her silver hair pulled into a bun, small gold hoops in her ears. Bourgeois had unfashionably declared that she made art because her emotions were bigger than herself.

Yes, it is sometimes agonizing to feel things. I had spent the last few months trying not to feel anything at all. Bourgeois had learned to sew at an early age in her parents' tapestry business. She thought of the needle as an object of psychological repair – and what she wanted to repair, she said, was the past.

We either die of the past or we become an artist.

Proust had reached for this same thought and came up with something that better suited this phase in my life:

Ideas come to us as the successors to griefs, and griefs, at
the moment when they change into ideas, lose some part
of their power to injure the heart.

As I battled with the moths and various griefs and the past, all of which returned every day to torment me, I glanced again at these two artists placed askew on the fridge door. To my eyes, the particular quality of their attention as they calmly shaped the forms they were inventing gave them beauty without measure. That kind of beauty was all that mattered to me. At this uncertain time, writing was one of the few activities in which I could handle the anxiety of uncertainty, of not knowing what was going to happen next. An idea presented itself, came my way, perhaps hatched from a grief, but I did not know if it would survive my free-floating attention, never mind my more focused attention. To unfold any number of ideas through all the dimensions of time is the great adventure of the writing life. But I had nowhere to write.

FIVE

GRAVITY

Celia came to the rescue. She was an actor and book-seller in her early eighties. One evening in her kitchen in late January, she started to sing something to me in Welsh. I told her I didn't understand Welsh.

'Well, I was born in Wales and you weren't, but what I was thinking while I was singing is that you need a place to write.'

She pointed towards the shed at the back of her garden. It was where her husband, the late, great poet Adrian Mitchell, had sometimes written in the spring and summer. It was built under an apple tree. In three seconds flat, I agreed to rent it from her. Celia knew I was financially supporting 'quite a crowd', as she put it, so we sealed a manageable deal over a glass of the Havana rum she had a liking for, and which she preferred to mix with Coke. Every time she drank Havana rum, she raised her glass to toast the miracle of the high literacy rate in Cuba. 'By the way,' she said, 'next time the communal boiler is on the blink in your flat, you'd better all come over for a hot bath.'

Everyone deserves a guardian angel like Celia.

It was not a posh shed. The lawnmower would have felt at home in it, but it did have four windows looking out on to the garden, a writing desk that had belonged to Adrian with a green leather top, and some Formica bookshelves built across the back wall. I was also to live with the ashes of the golden Labrador, known to many of Adrian's readers as Daisy the Dog of Peace.

Celia said, 'Well, you can get a lot of books on those shelves but I'm not going to unsettle Daisy.' In fact, she had acquired a new one-eyed dog from a rescue home. This tiny hound barked ferociously every time I walked into the house. Celia, who was a lifelong pacifist, wondered if I should be armed with a water pistol to teach her dog to lay off me. She went out and bought a set of three plastic pistols from the 99p shop, but in the end I started to use the garden door at the side of the house to get to the shed. Celia understood that I would be writing at all hours, and introduced me to her many friends as She Who Lurks in the Garden. No one was allowed to interrupt me on her watch; to knock on the door and solicit a conversation (the weather, the news, the arrival of cake) or even to convey an urgent message from the Mistress of the House. To be valued and respected in this way, as if it were the most normal thing in the world, was a new experience. I did not know it then, but I would go on to write three books in that shed, including the one you are reading now. It was there that I would begin to write in the first person, using an *I* that is close to myself and yet is not myself.

My guardian angel, who was fierce and loved to shout at everyone – when she wasn't shouting at a demonstration to save the National Health Service – insisted on keeping her *extra* freezer in the shed. There were times when the only things in that freezer, which came up to my waist, were twenty plastic tubs of quartered apples, gathered from the tree in autumn. It was Celia's pleasure to bake apple crumble throughout the year, while Myvy the One-Eyed Dog of War leaned against her ankles in total devotion. It wouldn't have surprised me if that scruffy hound started to sing in Welsh.

I told Celia that Freud was intrigued by how in dreams it was his patients most invested in appearing to be rational who were happiest when a dog quoted a line of poetry. She said that if Myvy was ever going to recite poetry, it would have to be written by Adrian. Apparently, Myvy's full Welsh name was Myfanwy, meaning My Dearest, though it could also mean My Rare One, My Woman, or My Beloved. I thought it best not to throw more of Freud her way while she had a knife in her hand.

Dogs love their friends and bite their enemies, quite unlike people, who are incapable of pure love and always have to mix love and hate in their object-relations.

Later, when I experienced my first autumn in that shed, the apples would crash from the tree on to the roof. It was an explosive sound. I began to understand why Newton nailed his theory on gravity by watching the way an apple falls so irrevocably. There is no such thing as an apple falling slowly.

The day I moved into the shed, it was snowing. The freezer wheezed its cold vapours. There were spiderwebs on the roof, dust on everything, leaves and mud on the floor. How was I to make a viable space to write in winter? Writing a novel requires many hours of sitting still, as if on a long-haul flight, final destination unknown, but a route of sorts mapped out. I draped two sheepskin rugs over my writing chair. It looked vaguely Stone Age. I set up my desktop computer, figured out the available plugs in the walls and then brought in the extension leads. While the snow fell on the apple tree, I sat on the floor untangling wires and sorting out the boxes of my journals and books. I wondered what to do with all the paper that accompanies a writer of my generation. There were scripts for theatre and film, poems, stories, libretti for opera, drafts of novels that had been written on a number of technologies – the manual typewriter, the electric typewriter, early computers. Some of my diaries dated back to 1985. One of them was scrawled with a long riff, written when I was twenty-six, featuring the word *it*.

It begins with knowing and not knowing, a glass of milk, rain, a reproach, a door slammed shut, a mother's sharp tongue, a snail, a wish, bitten fingernails, an open window. Sometimes it is easy and sometimes it is unbearable.

What was *it*? I don't know. But the glass of milk is a clue. It might have been the first beginnings of a novel I was going to write later in this shed, and which I would title *Hot Milk*. There were two journals that recorded meeting the man I was going to marry and my certainty that we were fated for each other. At the time, I could not see the point of my life without him. I realized when reading these journals that we had almost no life together before we had children. One year into our romance, we were living together and I was pregnant.

This was a joyful discovery. We sowed grass seed in the small garden of the house we were renting so that it would grow in time for the arrival of our first daughter.

In the meanwhile, I had to use all my ingenuity to heat the apartment on the hill when the communal boilers from the 1930s refused to cooperate with the twenty-first century, and I had to heat the shed. Of course I wanted to instal a wood-burning stove in the shed (what was I to do with the freezer?) and live a romantic writer's life – preferably Lord Byron's life, writing poetry in a velvet smoking jacket, waiting for inspiration to ravish me as the fragrant wood crackled and popped, etc. Alas, at this financially austere time it was not possible, but as Celia pointed out, 'Staring into the flames doesn't help the word count anyway.' I could see her point. The writing life is mostly about stamina. To get to the finishing line requires the writing to become more interesting than everyday life, and a log fire, like everyday life, is never boring.

It was my great fortune that Celia had become alarmed at the arctic weather and bought herself a portable gas heater in the style of a Provençal wood-burning stove. It was made from thick cast iron and massively heavy, the gas bottle discreetly hidden within its cast-iron body. I think it was supposed to resemble an old-fashioned wood burner in a grand French nineteenth-century farmhouse. Celia had it on full flame in her kitchen, along with the central heating. When she began to come down to lunch in shorts and a T-shirt and felt too limp and faint to shout at anyone, she knew it had to move to the shed. It was a very impractical and possibly dangerous heater for a small shed, what with the freezer rumbling away. At first I thought I would have the Provençal imposter transported up the hill to my flat, but the communal boilers were now on the mend.

The climate in the shed began to resemble a humid coastal resort in the tropics. I brought in a flask of tea and sipped it through the day as the blue flames flickered and snow fell on the apple tree. The appeal of writing, as I understood it, was an invitation to climb in-between the apparent reality of things, to see not only the tree but the insects that live in its infrastructure, to discover that everything is connected in the ecology of language and living. 'Ecology' from the Greek for house or for living relations. It doesn't take more than three months of living to discover that we are all connected to each other's cruelty and to each other's kindness.

The stylish heater reminded me of the uglier gas fires we used to heat the draughty rehearsal rooms in the days I wrote plays. We rehearsed long hours, chain-smoked, drank instant coffee, then stumbled home late at night with a blinding head-ache. When we were rehearsing a play I had written, titled *Macbeth False Memories*, we had a dinosaur gas heater on the go. The director had made the leading actor repeat one particular monologue at least twelve times. He was playing the part of an Italian entrepreneur, Lavelli, who was an avatar for many of the themes that I was going to push into my fiction. Lavelli was in the business of detecting forged banknotes and credit cards. He was later murdered by his colleague, a depressed, emotionally numb man called Bennet.

> LAVELLI: Mr Bennet, show me a credit card and I will tell you in seconds if it is a forgery. The artist may correct his canvas fifty times, but the forger, if he is good, corrects his imitation only twice. He has to paint in *the manner of the original.* And I have some respect for him. Those of us who cannot imitate lack imagination. We cannot see outside our own manner . . . we are nasty little nationalists. The foreigner, the stranger, he too must learn to make a forgery of himself. He must imitate the host culture. We are supposed to value originality, but the truth is we want to be like each other. We even want our differences to be the same differences. You still with me, Bennet?
>
> BENNET: Um, Yes.

By the time Bennet said, 'Um, yes,' everyone in the rehearsal room was more or less asphyxiated from the gas fumes. I had learned that an actor can convey a great deal with just two words. Lavelli was a clever and reflective trickster, a man at ease with language. He was tormenting Bennet, who, as the audience knew, was completely out of his depth.

It was calm and silent and dark in my shed. I had let go of the life I had planned and was probably out of my depth every day. It's hard to write and be open and let things in when life is tough, but to keep everything out means there's nothing to work with. I had decided to take ten key books with me to the shed, including the poetry of Apollinaire, Éluard, Plath and Emily Dickinson (whose spirit flew to me that night via the bees), a book on the anatomy of the human body, and Robert Graves on myth. This meant the bookshelves were mostly empty, but I did not want to recreate a version of my orderly former study in the dusty shed.

Was it a shed or a hut? The philosopher Martin Heidegger had called his shed *die Hütte*. I looked it up on Google and gazed at a photograph of him sitting thoughtfully on a bench in his three-roomed hut. It was built in the Black Forest mountains of southern Germany. His wife, Elfride Heidegger, a former economics student, stood bent over two cooking pots on the stove. They both looked joyless, grey and grim. Apparently, many of Heidegger's great works of philosophy were written in the hut, including *Being and Time*, published in 1927. It was one of the books I had brought with me to the shed. I had made a bracket in red felt tip to hold this sentence:

'Everyone is the other and no one is himself.' Um. Yes. In a sense, it is what Lavelli was trying to convey to Bennet in my early script. Every time I read Heidegger in my hut, I realized that I was Bennet.

At the end of the day I would begin the long walk up one of the highest hills in London to cook supper for my daughter. Sometimes I stopped to get my breath back by the gates of the local cemetery. It was such a long walk in the dark. The night smelt of moss and the wet marble of the gravestones. I did not feel safe or unsafe, but somewhere in-between, liminal, passing from one life to another.

Six

THE BODY ELECTRIC

I bought an electric bicycle to help me get up the hill. It was heavy, a tank of a bike, but with the wind behind me I could overtake a moped. My e-bike was the best thing that had happened to me in a long while. I could zip from one place to another in no time at all. I rode it fast. I cursed and shouted at drivers when they opened their front doors in a way that toppled me on to the road. I had road rage. Yes, I had graduated to road rage on my electric bicycle. That is to say, I had a lot of rage from my old life and it expressed itself on the road. I would cycle up the hill with heavy bags of groceries and a box of fruit on the back rack. With the help of my electric bike I began to feel as if I was on a mini vacation from the melancholy of the last few months. As I cycled fast down the long Holloway Road, for some reason the stretch of tarmac reminded me of the dark brooding Adriatic Sea in Trieste.

Perhaps it was a sense that something dangerous lurked beneath it, but I figured that the crash had already happened when the boat that was my marriage hit the rocks, and anyway, why not stop thinking about it and concentrate on the idea that the Holloway Road, with its bus lanes and traffic jams, could also be the Adriatic Sea.

I usually locked up my bike in the back car park of my crumbling apartment block. Other residents parked their motorbikes there. On the days I lugged home many bags of shopping, I would park the bike behind a tree in the front car park to unload the bags. I would then carry the bags into the lobby and leave them outside the lift. Then I would ride the bike to the back car park, lock it and walk back to the front car park to load the groceries into the lift and take them to the sixth floor. A middle-aged resident of my apartment block, a woman called Jean, insisted I could not park my bike in the front car park.

Not even behind a tree. Not even for two minutes. She had a sweet, high-pitched voice. The voice of a wolf softening its rough feral voice to trick the baby goats into opening the door so she could eat them up. Where was their mother? Probably at work earning a living. Jean had made it her mission to always be standing by my bike in her colourful cardigan on the very days I unloaded my groceries. There she was, leaning on the handlebars, smiling while she said nasty things in her sweet voice. It was important to Jean to convey that it was more in sorrow than in anger that she made my life even more difficult.

On one occasion, when I was unloading the groceries in a rush, Jean suddenly appeared from behind the tree, like a scene in an Ealing comedy. 'Ah,' she said, 'you are always in such a hurry. Busy busy busy all the time.'

Jean had too much time on her hands. She was hysterically happy and I was calmly miserable. As she stood watching me lift six bags, the string of pearls I wore round my neck burst apart and fell to the ground, bouncing towards Joan's sensible shoes.

'Oh dear,' her lips parted to show an abundance of little white teeth, 'Tuesday is not your day, is it?'

On a Tuesday some years ago, I had gone to the cinema with the father of my children to see the film *A.I. Artificial Intelligence* by Steven Spielberg. We sat next to each other in the dark, close but separate. The film was about a robot boy made in a laboratory who was special because he was programmed to be able to love. His adopted mother grew frightened of her robot son's affection and abandoned him in the woods. Thousands of years later, the robot boy is discovered at the bottom of a frozen river by strange and beautiful creatures that are artificial life. They have tall, thin bodies, similar to the figures in early cave paintings, and they are very respectful to the boy robot. They realize he is their last contact with human beings because it was a human who programmed him. It was during that film that I knew our marriage was over. We also needed to find the robot boy because he was programmed to love. He had something inside him that we needed to be inside us.

'You're right,' I said to Jean, 'Tuesday is not my day.'

When I told Celia about Jean, she said, 'Next time she hassles you, tell her that you're not getting any younger.' I was slightly shocked when she said that. When I left her kitchen that night after the usual small glass of best Havana rum, I heard her whisper to one of her friends, 'I don't understand why she wears pearls to write in that dusty old shed anyway.' My best male friend, who was about to get married for the third time, could not understand why I did not tell Jean to fuck off. I asked him what he was going to wear to his third wedding? He was apparently tempted to splash out on a bright yellow jacket he had spotted in a designer shop in Carnaby Street.

'Whatever you do,' I said, 'steer away from yellow.'

'Maybe,' he replied, 'I'll ask my *wife* what *she* thinks. By the way, how's it going? Have they fixed The Corridors of Love yet?'

'No, the corridors are still waiting to be restored. Apart from that, I enjoy every day. My life is full of my daughters and their friends. There's lots of shouting and hormonal stormy weather all round and doors slamming regularly and many bills. By the way, does your new wife have a name?'

'*You* know her name is Nadia,' he said.

He made us both an omelette and then, as a serial husband, wanted to know more about why I did not swim back to the leaking boat that was my marriage.

'Well, why would I swim back to a boat that is going to crash and sink?' I asked.

'It offers symbolic protection,' he said, glancing through the prongs of his fork at the band of gold on his finger.

The next time Jean stopped me on my bike, I smiled right back at her.

'You know, it is very heavy to carry all this stuff up from the back car park and I am not getting any younger.' I couldn't believe I had said those words in that nice understanding tone. Jean blinked and mentally swallowed another five jars of honey. Then she said, 'Well, as you're busy busy busy, have you thought of getting the supermarket to deliver your shopping?'

There was something that made me resist the supermarket delivering my shopping. It was a slog to carry it up the hill on my bike, but I enjoyed the slog. I wanted to choose my fish and herbs and winter vegetables and also I was very proud of something my father had taught me, which was a way of checking that certain kinds of fruit, such as melon or papaya, were ripe. This involved, he said, pressing my fingertips into both ends of the fruit, very lightly so as not to bruise the flesh, and if it was ripe the extremities of the fruit would have the texture of a *firm* earlobe. It never failed. No, I did not want my fruit delivered in a refrigerated van. Could I ask the driver to compare the fruit I had bought online to the human ear?

Those words 'I am not getting any younger' had calmed Jean down. Yet there was a part of me that wondered if it would have been *calming* to explain to her that I had a full professional life and a full mothering life and a minor plumbing life. What was it that needed calming in Jean? Why all that strained smiling? It was as if she felt ashamed to be living alone and was transmitting a portion of that shame to me. If she had reluctantly stepped outside the societal story that offered her symbolic protection, how was she to protect herself? The newspaper she read every day had no respect for her, in fact it hated her, but she was addicted to being hated.

What is a woman for? What should a woman be? What was it that Jean needed me to be? Or not to be? That was the question I had no time to ask her. As she had told me, more in anger than in sorrow, I was busy earning a living, even on sad Tuesdays.

I became obsessed with my electric bicycle. I had *wheels*. One night I rode it to a party at least twenty miles away. I whizzed along the roads with my dress flying in the wind behind me. It was hard not to whoop. Perhaps my children and my e-bike were my only happiness. When I walked into the party, a tall man with silver hair came to talk to me. He told me he wrote military biographies, mostly about the First World War, and asked me to pass him a canapé.

I was unlacing my trainers to swap for the more glamorous shoes I had brought with me, and ignored his request, although lifting a canapé off the silver tray would have been a breeze after all the usual heavy lifting.

He was tall and thin, possibly in his late sixties, and seemed to desire my company. He talked about his books for a while and how his wife (no name) was unwell at home. He did not ask me one single question, not even my name. It seemed that what he needed was a devoted, enchanting woman at his side to acquire his canapés for him and who understood that he was entirely the subject. What with his silver hair and silver eyebrows, I started to think of him as the Big Silver. If he stepped out of character and asked me a few questions, what would I actually say to the Big Silver? If he asked the obligatory 'So what do you do?' I suppose I could see him off by telling the truth.

'As you've asked, I spent today engaged with the difficulties of writing in the immediate present tense. It's hard to remain interested in one person's subjectivity. There are tricks to insert other subjectivities into this tense but it's a challenge.'

No, I would never begin that kind of conversation with the Big Silver. I was re-reading the early novels and various essays and interviews by James Baldwin, and his title, *Nobody Knows My Name*, helped me understand why I objected to my male walking companion never remembering the names of women – same with my best male friend (also known as Bluebeard), whose wives were never referred to by their names until he divorced them. In an interview with Studs Terkel in the 1960s, Baldwin, talking about race in America, had laid down a challenge: 'in order to learn your name you are going to have to learn mine'. *Yes*, I thought, *what I should really say to the Big Silver is something like, 'You are going to have to learn my name so that I can learn yours.'* He would be mystified. To be frank, I was mystified. It was mysterious. Simone de Beauvoir described *The Second Sex* as an exposition of 'the pervasiveness and intensity and mysteriousness of the history of women's oppression'.

It is so mysterious to want to suppress women. It is even more mysterious when women want to suppress women. I can only think we are so very powerful that we need to be suppressed all the time. Anyway, like James Baldwin had taught me, I had to decide who I was and then convince everyone at the party that was who I was, but unfortunately in this phase, I was whistling in the dark. I had to survive my losses and find some rituals to celebrate them.

While the Big Silver continued talking about himself, I saw the man who cried at the funeral coming towards me. We embraced warmly, lingering for a while in that embrace to acknowledge the last time we had met in very charged circumstances – the funeral of his long-time lover, the end of my marriage.

'How are you?' he whispered in my ear.

'I don't know.'

'Yes, you do.'

'Well, okay,' I replied, 'this afternoon I had an argument with my copy-editor about commas. She is keen to insert more commas into my text for easy reading. She loves commas. Her affliction is nothing less than a comma psychosis. She inserts them everywhere. It is like working with a comma on Viagra.'

When the man who cried at the funeral laughed, it occurred to me that I had only heard him cry, which was an odd way round to meet someone.

We were both now talking over the Big Silver.

He said he had been reading Gertrude Stein's *Lectures in America.*

'Apparently Stein thought it is obvious when something is a question so she stopped using question marks and she thought that commas were servile. In her view it was up to the reader if they wanted to stop and take a breath.'

He leaned forward to lift two glasses of champagne off a silver tray and passed one of them to me.

It had taken him a while to recover from his ex-lover's shocking death, but a strange thing had happened. He told me that Love had not only signed the visitor's book, it had moved in. His name was Geoff. 'By the way,' he said, 'where's your pearl necklace? I thought you never took it off, even when you swim?' After I had told him about it exploding on my behalf in the front car park, he said, 'If you are doing all the heavy lifting, you should do something that's the opposite.'

'Like what?'

'Why don't you make ice cream?'

He took my arm and led me into the garden.

'Who is the man you were talking to with the silver hair?'

'He writes military biographies. War is his subject,' I said to my new friend, who had given up smoking but was nevertheless smoking.

'Ah,' he replied, waving his cigarette about, 'I wonder if he agrees with Brecht: "War is like love; it always finds a way." Aren't you cold in that dress?'

'No. I spend so much time outside I don't feel the cold any more.'

'I need a blanket if we're going to stand here.'

While he shivered and smoked, I told him about a sixty-year-old female masseuse who had recently pummelled my spine as I lay on my stomach with my face shoved into the hole in the massage bed. She had apparently spent the weekend buying soft blankets – very-good-quality mohair and hundred per cent wools – which she had laid over her sofa and chairs. When I asked her, 'Why blankets?', she said, 'Because the war is over.'

I had found myself guffawing with my face in that hole. She was laughing too. I wasn't sure what we were laughing about, except to guess she was alluding to making peace with an undisclosed hurt.

I would have liked to know more about her war. It was not won on the playing fields of Eton, that's for sure.

We could see that people had started to dance inside the house.

The man who cried at the funeral pushed me towards the door. 'Come on, your dress is so lovely, let's dance, let's dance, let's dance.'

We danced as if it was our very last night on earth – and to celebrate his new love and my new freedom and to celebrate my having been nominated for a big literary prize and to a thousand and one nights without pain, and because, as he put it, 'life is as fragile as a glass slipper'. I didn't quite get that, but he said he'd had too much champagne so maybe he meant a glass coffin – which was even more bewildering, but then he was The Man Who Cried at the Funeral.

We kicked off our shoes just like the song that was being played told us to do. Three luscious red velvet sofas had been pushed against the walls. We whirled and leapt around and sweated and then a striped kitten slunk on to the dance floor, like a tiny leopard, its tail raised. I gently lifted it up from the feet of the crowd and placed it on top of my new friend's head.

'I can feel it purring through my fingers,' he said. At that moment I thought the tempest was over. I was ready to do something I had never done before – like write a manifesto on the toilet wall in a pub.

I believe in people who are nervous and whose hands shake a little

The kitten had now escaped and was making its way towards the red velvet sofas, just as Bowie sang about falling and trembling and about a flower. I followed it and sat next to a woman with long black hair who was perched on the edge of one of the sofas. She was wearing a white shirt and was engrossed in sewing a small pearl button on to the left cuff. She was saying something to me, but I couldn't hear her that well because she had a needle in her mouth. My hair, which I always wore up, had come undone and I had a hairpin in my mouth. The man who cried at the funeral made his way towards us, very slowly and lightly, as if he were walking on a glass coffin.

'Hello Clara,' he said to the woman on the sofa, 'I would like you to meet my friend. Do you know she can put her hair up with just one pin?'

'Yes, I know how to do that too,' she said.

When I returned home, I spent an hour on the Internet in conversation with Gupta in India about my faulty Microsoft Word program.

When I next looked at my chat box, Gupta had written, *Don't worry. I am here to help you.*

For some reason, the letter *I* on the screen was blinking and jumping and trembling.

That's how I felt too.

SEVEN

THE BLACK AND BLUISH DARKNESS

My new life was all about fumbling for keys in the dark.

I had a key to my mother's house and a key for my daughter to get into her father's flat. There was a key to Celia's garden door that led to the writing shed and a key for the shed itself, a key to Celia's house, a key to my electric bicycle, a key for the e-battery, a key known as a fob to get into my own building and then two keys for the front door. It was February in Britain. The early morning sky was like midnight. It was dark again in the afternoon when I locked the shed and walked through the sodden garden carrying the bike battery (which had been charging during the day). Then I unlocked the garden door (a tricky door to open and close even in daylight), wheeled the bike and my bags out of the garden door and locked it again. Often Celia's car was parked in the driveway and it was near impossible to squeeze the bike past it. She was not getting any younger, given she was in her mid eighties, so I did not want to interrupt her from shouting at everyone in the house. Instead, I had to lift the whole heavy e-machine over the car bonnet without scraping off the paint.

I bought a torch and carried it with me everywhere. I was also enjoying my new electric screwdriver. It fitted perfectly into my purse and looked like a small revolver. There was something very satisfying about pressing the red button and listening to it whirr like a maniac. I tightened up the loose screws in the garden door and in my shed door. This made locking and unlocking the doors easier in the dark. What with the keys, the screwdriver, the torch, my bags heavy with books and groceries and extension leads, it took some doing, even on an e-bike, to cycle up the perilously icy hill.

One afternoon, I made my way from the writing shed to a meeting about a possible film option on one of my novels. I should have travelled by tube, but somehow my bike was looking particularly seductive, standing tall and strong under the apple tree. At Mornington Crescent, I was obliged to turn the bike upside down on the pavement and attend to the links of the chain, which had jammed.

My hands were covered in black oil and I'd had to run into a noodle bar, buy a pot of green tea and then wash my hands in the toilet; no mirror, no soap, no hot water. It was very important not to be late for this meeting. There were school trips to pay for and a gas bill and also the horror of my computer starting to make strange clicking sounds when it refused to shut down.

The executives sat around a polished oak table in a window-less room. They were intelligent, experienced, groomed, at the top of their game. I was offered a glass of water and accepted it gratefully. After a while, I realized I had an old-fashioned idea of what a meeting such as this one should be like, and I had acquired it from watching too many black and white movies. What I had in mind was an atmosphere in which we sipped negronis in a nightclub in Rome, plotting the main arc of the film while dancers adorned in feathers cavorted in the background.

I was asked an important question. Who did I consider to be the main character in my novel *Swimming Home* – Kitty Finch or Jozef Nowogrodzki, also known as Joe? I replied that if it was Joe's film, the scriptwriter might be obliged to rather liter-ally fill in his back story (born in Poland, Jewish, smuggled through a forest in 1943 age five en route to East London) but that it would be more interesting to give the task of tracking his back story to Kitty Finch, who anyway believed she was in telepathy with him. I suggested that I should write the screen-play because I knew how to unfold this back story from Kitty's point of view. 'We don't need to tell the past through flashback,' I said, but when asked to explain how I might reveal the past in another way, I found myself stuck for words.

Actually, the coexisting past and present was a technique I was starting to develop in my fiction, and I could see how it might work in film. They clearly didn't believe me and asked me to email them a list of minor and major characters by the end of the week.

After the meeting I made my way to a café for a much-needed espresso. There was a large mirror in a baroque gold frame hanging on the wall. This is where I discovered that I had sat through that meeting with three small muddy leaves stuck in my hair. I think this was because I'd had to duck under the apple tree to get out of the shed. It was not a good look, but it could have been worse: spiderwebs trailing on the edges of my ears, small dead bugs hanging from my eyebrows. Working in a shed had its problems when it came to grooming. And so did riding an electric bike. In a sense it was the main character in my life.

It was such hard work. The main character is always the hardest work.

My e-bike was more demanding than my children. Earlier, on my way to the meeting, two different men had stopped to ask about my e-bike, one at the traffic lights at Camden Town, one by the fruit stall outside Goodge Street station. I had wheeled the bike over to this stall to buy one single purple plum. At first I thought these pleasant men were just finding an excuse to speak to me because I was incredibly attractive to them, but no, I was the minor character and the e-bike was a countercultural celebrity. I suppose the men were minor characters and I had stepped outside my character, happy to explain that the maximum assisted speed was 15mph and it was fitted with a motor of 200 watts. While I talked to them, I felt I had joined a kind of brotherhood, while at the same time struggling with motherhood. I was an e-matriarch in a patriarchal reality. Life was hard and I had no script. *Perhaps I was writing one.* And what had happened to the plum? I had bitten into it while I spoke to the man at Goodge Street station. It was juicy, firm and plump. If I was writing the script, that plum would be a turning point in the plot – the man would have said, 'By the way, do you know there are three leaves stuck in your hair?'

I knocked back the espresso and stood up to continue with my day. Whatever, it was essential to add a compact mirror to my bag, along with the lipstick, electric screwdriver, fountain pen, torch and the small bottle of essential oil of rose (*Rosa centifolia*), which I was now applying to my wrists to make me feel calmer.

Does serenity smell like a rose? A rose is kind-hearted. A rose is consoling. The rose is the empress of the pinks. Perhaps a rose is the empress of the blues. When Bessie Smith sang about not being able to live in a house that was falling down, that's how I felt about my old life. It is also the song that James Baldwin listened to one winter in the mountains of Switzerland, where far away from Harlem he wrote *Nobody Knows My Name*.

Actually, I had no idea what serenity felt like. Serenity is supposed to be one of the main characters in old-fashioned femininity's cultural personality. She is serene and she endures. Yes, she is so talented at enduring and suffering they might even be the main characters in her story.

It was possible that femininity, as I had been taught it, had come to an end. Femininity, as a cultural personality, was no longer expressive for me. It was obvious that femininity, as written by men and performed by women, was the exhausted phantom that still haunted the early twenty-first century.

What would it cost to step out of character and stop the story? There were many variations of course, including corporate femininity, in which women with male bosses were still required to dress in a way that gave a nod to the boardroom and the bedroom. How was it possible to be erotically and commercially switched on for your boss all the time? That sort of femininity does not wear very well. After a while it starts to show the dirt. My friend Sasha, who was financially thriving, had told me that on Fridays she and her female work colleagues ended the week by getting blind drunk in various bars and vomiting all over their corporate uniforms. I thought Sasha and her friends were late capitalism's version of the maenads, female followers of Dionysus also known as the 'raving ones', except they wore bull helmets and could tear up sturdy trees when intoxicated. In fifth-century-BC Athens their bodies were imaginatively possessed by various gods. Sasha pointed out that in the twenty-first century, her body was imaginatively possessed by her various male bosses – who insisted that wearing high heels and short skirts to work was incredibly empowering.

No, there were not that many women I knew who wanted to put the phantom of femininity together again. What is a phantom anyway? The phantom of femininity is an illusion, a delusion, a societal hallucination. She is a very tricky character to play and it is a role (sacrifice, endurance, cheerful suffering) that has made some women go mad. This was not a story I wanted to hear all over again.

It was time to find new main characters with other talents.

As I walked towards my e-bike, which I had locked up outside a Tesco Express, I groaned at the disaster of that meeting. How was I going to conquer the film world if I sauntered into the executive suite with leaves in my hair? How was I going to get a break if I couldn't find words to explain a technique for flashback in the present tense that I had learned from film in the first place? Directors such as David Lynch, Michael Haneke, Agnès Varda and Alain Resnais were my muses and teachers in this regard. And in particular the films of Marguerite Duras, mostly because of the ways she cinematically revealed the return of repressed memory in the lives of her screen protagonists. She had made a language in film that cut as close to human subjectivity as it is possible to get without dying of pain.

Somehow I had repressed that information in the windowless executive suite.

One of my own undiscovered talents, I was convinced, was to be a scriptwriter. Everyone I knew was bored with the same old performance of masculinity and femininity written for the major and minor characters. I flash-forwarded to my seventies, and saw myself typing at the edge of my swimming pool in California. I would be a legendary sun-damaged genius of cinema, known for typing in my swimming costume, surrounded by verdant tropical plants which always open the mind and make something happen. At lunchtime my staff would shake up my cocktail and toss fresh squid on the barbecue.

It had started to rain. The London pavements smelt of old coins.

Yes, my sunlit garden in California would be full of chirping colourful birds. The bird clock in my London apartment was just a rehearsal for the real thing. At the end of the day, shattered from finding techniques to haul the past into the present tense without a single flashback, I would swim in the moonlight with my chosen companion – while all the minor and major characters in my film script patiently waited for me to greet them in the morning. Was my chosen companion a minor or major character? Major, obviously. And where were my children? Oh no! They would be grown up, living their own lives, dreading a call from their mother – *It's her, she's in California.*

And what could I say to my daughters? 'Um, I'm not like those mothers who lived through you, no no, not at all. I have a major character in the pool with me. I am living a full exciting life. By the way, what are you doing for Christmas? You know the climate is *tropical* here?'

I walked into Tesco Express and bought a chicken to roast for my daughter and her friends. As a second thought, I also purchased a single sprig of rosemary in a small sealed bag.

That night as I cycled up the hill in the pouring rain, my bag split open and out of it spilled a book by Freud, *Jokes and Their Relation to the Unconscious*, the charger to my electric bike battery (instructions: *do not expose to rain*), a lipstick, a torch, a screwdriver and five tangerines. The traffic had to stop while I looked for the chicken. It was lying like roadkill near the wheels of the car that had run it over, flattened but intact, its skin imprinted with the marks of the tyre. I picked it up and let the tangerines roll down the hill.

While I smashed garlic and lemons into a paste to mari-nate the chicken that had been killed twice, once in a slaughterhouse and once on a London road, I realized my clothes were soaked from the rain. I was truly exhausted and I was alone. There was no adult around to say, 'Why don't you take off those wet clothes and have a hot shower?' I was alone and I was free. Free to pay the immense service charges for an apartment that had very little service and sometimes not even basic utilities. Free to support my family by writing on a computer that was about to die. It was urgent that I made that list of minor and major characters and emailed it to the executive suite without delay.

I slammed the chicken into the oven and wondered if I should open the bottle of wine that had been a gift from the man who cried at the funeral. At the same time, I glimpsed the lone sprig of rosemary I had bought at the supermarket, the barcode stamped on the sealed bag. Rosemary was the herb for remembrance, but all I wanted to do was forget. At the family house, I had planted rosemary in the sunniest part of the garden. It had grown into a lush flowering shrub with violet-blue flowers. The solitary sprig in front of me was a bullet to the past.

I decided to open the wine and texted my friend Lily to come over and share it with me. She arrived with a box of strawberries and ran me a bath while she talked about her day. My daughter and her teenage friends laid the table. They wore big hoop earrings and lip gloss. They were crazed by life and crazed for life. Their conversation was interesting, astute and hilarious. I thought they could save the world. Everything else fell away, like the flesh from the run-over chicken, which my daughter and her friends and Lily and I devoured with relish.

Eight

THE REPUBLIC

To separate from love is to live a risk-free life. What's the point of that sort of life? As I wheeled my electric bike through the park on the way to my writing shed, my hands had turned blue from the cold. I had given up wearing gloves because I was always grappling in the dark for keys. I stopped by the fountain, only to find it had been switched off. A sign from the council read, *This fountain has been winterized.*

I reckoned that is what had happened to me too.

To live without love is a waste of time. I was living in the Republic of Writing and Children. I was not Simone de Beauvoir, after all. No, I had got off the train at a different stop (marriage) and stepped on to a different platform (children). She was my muse but I was certainly not hers.

All the same we had both bought a ticket (earned with our own money) for the same train. The destination was to head towards a freer life. That is a vague destination, no one knows what it looks like when we get there. It is a journey without end, but I did not know that then. I was just on my way. Where else was there to head for? I was young and lovely, I boarded that train, opened my journal and began to write in the first person and the third person.

Simone de Beauvoir knew that a life without love was a waste of time. Her enduring love for Sartre seems to have been contingent on her living in hotels and not making a home with him, which in the 1950s was more radical than I believe even she realized. She remained committed to Sartre being the essential love of her life for fifty-one years, despite their other attachments. She knew she never wanted children or to serve his breakfast or run his errands or pretend she was not intellectually engaged with the world to make herself more loveable to him. She was appalled by middle age, in ways I did not completely understand. All the same, as she had written to the writer Nelson Algren, in the flush of their new love, 'I want everything from life, I want to be a woman and to be a man, to have many friends and have loneliness, to work much and write good books and to travel and enjoy myself . . .'

When I was on a book tour in America and landed in Chicago, I was assigned a driver by my publisher. His name was Bill and he knew everything about Chicago. The first thing Bill did was drive me to see where Nelson Algren had lived when Simone de Beauvoir made the long journey from France to be in his arms. It was a leafy road, lined with spacious houses built from red brick, with verandas and gardens. Bill told me that in Algren's day it was a rough, grimy neighbourhood and that Algren hung out with whores, boxers and junkies. I thought of Simone, one of the leading intellectuals of her era, arriving in Chicago, as different from Paris as it could possibly be, and how she found love on the third floor of that old red-brick house. For a while, Algren had emotionally and sexually freed her from Sartre.

What was it like to not wake up in a hotel? To be a guest in her lover's *home*? Presumably he had chosen some furniture and bought his own light bulbs. He was her host. Algren had written to her when he feared their transatlantic love affair was ending, to tell her the truth about the things he wanted: 'a place of my own to live in, with a woman of my own and perhaps a child of my own. There's nothing extraordinary about wanting such things.'

No, there is nothing extraordinary about all those nice things. Except that she knew it would cost her more than it would cost him. In the end she decided she couldn't afford it. When Algren begged her to leave Paris and live with him in Chicago, she wrote, 'I could not live just for happiness and love. I could not give up writing and working in the only place where my writing and work may have meaning.'

Surely she could write and have happiness and love and a home and a child? She didn't think so. I had found it quite tricky myself. All the same, I did know from a young age that if I chose to, I could take authorial control of my books. This is not as obvious as it sounds. How was I going to do that in my twenties if I was supposed to please everyone all the time in a bid for approval, home, children and love?

And what about the men who, like Algren, wanted home, children and love? In my Boston hotel, I had glimpsed a man sitting with his female companion at a café table overlooking the harbour. He was in love with her, attentive and gentle and kind. She had taken off her sandals and jacket and sunglasses and the gold bracelet on her wrist. While he pressed his lips against the glowing skin of her bare arms, she looked into the distance, and then walked away from his lips and from the sunshine. After a while, he gathered up her sandals, bracelet, sunglasses and bag, his camera, sun cream and phone, and made his way to the table in the shade. Something or someone in his life had made him brave enough to do all the carrying and all the kissing. If he wanted her more than she wanted him, how would she begin that conversation in a way that did not destroy his courage?

While I sat on the stone steps by the winterized fountain, I saw one of my students walking through the park. She was wearing a red coat and red woollen gloves. She was speaking to someone on her phone. After a while she took the glove off her right hand to better grip the phone, reaching with her left hand for the few leaves left on the tree.

She had recently given me some of her writing to read. It was clear that she feared her emerging voice would be mocked. Every time she wrote something she really meant, she followed it with a self-deprecating joke to undermine the truth she had struggled to untangle. Perhaps this was a bid for approval, or a bid for love? Yet what sort of love would demand that she conceal her talent? Among her influences were Claude Cahun (born Lucy Schwob, poet, artist and resistance fighter in the Second World War), and a book she carried with her at all times, *Black Skin, White Masks,* by the psychiatrist and revolutionary Frantz Fanon, who was born on the Caribbean island Martinique. She had torn the wallpaper off the walls of her family house and slipped her hand inside the naked bricks to reach for something she knew was there. A feature of her story involved two caged singing birds. After I had read it a few times, I questioned these singing birds – to which she was very attached. The traumatic events in her writing occurred during the months of the monsoon in southern India, between July and September. I suggested she work with the rain instead of the birds. She rewrote the story and it came to life. It was both nuanced and furious – a hard combination to pull off. She had used the last line of a Langston Hughes poem as an ironic and sad refrain, which she had repeated throughout the story.

And I love the rain.

Now that the birds no longer screamed over her own powerful voice, the student told me it was hard to own up to its force. It scared her. When I told her that I believed she had an abundance of talent, she began to cry. And then she said, 'Sorry, I haven't had breakfast.' She fumbled in her rucksack and took out two tiny samosas. When she unravelled the napkin they were wrapped in and used it to wipe her eyes, she was nervous and her hands were shaking a little. Later in the day, I saw that she had left the samosas on my office desk. I'd had to run down two flights of stairs to find her, and when I placed them in her hand she looked at me and said, 'Oh, but I left them for you.'

'Well, thank you,' I replied. 'But you don't have to give me things for letting you know you're a genius.'

Marguerite Duras did not have the 'fatal patience' that de Beauvoir rightly thought women who were mothers had learned to their detriment. After Duras wrote *Lol Stein*, she made a curious remark – she said that she gave herself permission to speak 'in a sense totally alien to women'. I know what she means. It is so hard to claim our desires and so much more relaxing to mock them.

The student saw me standing by the switched-off fountain and waved. After we had exchanged the usual small talk – *What are you doing here, do you live near by* ? – I showed her the sign that said the fountain had been winterized. She asked me if that was a real word? I hadn't heard of it either. Was it a new verb? We looked it up on our phones and saw that it meant 'to adapt something for winter'. In that case, I wasn't winterized after all. I identified with Camus, who declared he had an invincible summer inside him, even in winter. I was still exploring the idea that the Holloway Road resembled the Adriatic Sea. I hadn't done with that notion yet, but it was hard to pull it home. The student told me that she had recently seen an exhibition by the American photographer Francesca Woodman. Woodman had made a series of self-portraits, often naked, in which she had found a technique to blur the female form. She was always trying to make herself disappear into walls and behind the wallpaper and into floors, to become vapour, a spectre, a smudge, a blur, a female subject that is erased but recognizable.

'Yes,' she said, 'I often feel like that.'

'At least you've got yourself some gloves,' I quipped. 'That way, you are winterized.'

After a while I asked her where she was heading.

It turned out that she was going to have breakfast with her friend Nisha, who happened to be a photographer.

'We're broke so we order one full English. Nisha takes the bacon, sausage and one egg, I take the mushrooms, tomato and the other egg, we share the beans and hash potato.'

'That sounds like a good arrangement,' I said, 'but isn't the hash potato American?'

'Yeah, it's a full English with a special relationship with America. But to be honest I prefer a hash brownie to a hash potato.'

We wished each other a good day and I made my way down the hill to my writing shed.

The shed was winterized. It was now warm. I had laid down two kelim rugs on the floor, but I had no desire to domesticate my workspace. So far, apart from ten books, my computer and various journals, there was not much else in my shed.

A candle in the shape of a cactus.

The ashes of Daisy the Dog of Peace.

A Mexican mirror framed with small ceramic tiles.

A blue wooden chair.

A green writing chair covered in two sheepskins.

The freezer.

A long lamp with a concrete circular base and a silver-tipped bulb.

A green and yellow striped umbrella.

A packet of nuts and raisins.

A radio.

The gardener who came once a month to look after the apple tree and plants was an actor in his mid fifties. He had a deep calming voice and the bluest eyes. We often spoke about books we were reading and his various acting jobs and why we had chosen such precarious occupations. He seemed concerned that the shed was a stern, austere place to work in winter. Sometimes he'd pick a small bunch of herbs and winter flowers from the garden and bring them to me in the shed. I could not tell him that it was flowers that triggered some of the most painful flashbacks to my old life. How can a flower inflame a wound? It can and it does if it is a portal to the past. How can a flower reveal information about minor and major characters? It can and it does. How is it that a flower can resemble a criminal? For the writer and criminal Jean Genet, the striped uniform of convicts reminded him of flowers. Both flowers and flags are required to do so much of the talking for us, but I am not really sure I know what it is they are saying.

A gardener is always a futurist with a vision of how a small, humble plant will spring up and blaze in time. Do futurists have flashbacks or do they just flash-forward? I liked to think that the past, as I experienced it, came to the same end as Ziggy Stardust. I saw it off and then rose from the dead in a number of incredible outfits. Yes, I was with Ziggy *and* I was with Kierkegaard all the way: 'Life can only be understood backwards; but it must be lived forwards.'

In our various breaks from writing and gardening, he'd walk me around the different kinds of mint he was growing in pots, or talk through why he was so severely pruning the apple tree. I had become fond of this tree, not least because of the inspiring way the squirrels who scampered up and down the trunk would suddenly turn their gaze towards me, as I sat alone in the shed. Although they appeared to be startled, I knew they knew I was there *before* they turned to look. This had been my theme in *Things I Don't Want to Know*, in which I speculated that the things we don't want to know are the things that are known to us anyway, but we do not wish to look at them too closely. Freud described this wish to unknow what we know as motivated forgetting.

I was pleased to share this garden with the squirrels. I had spent two decades finding plants that would be hospitable to birds and bees and butterflies in our family home, but in this time of rupture, I just wanted a writing desk and a chair in the solitude of my hut.

This gardener had the knack of appearing to give everyone he spoke to all his attention, as if he was tending to a plant, assessing how it would respond to weather, to soil, to coexisting with other plants. I could tell from his intense blue gaze that he was an actor. He was curious about everything and

everyone. Acting is a strange job in which the actor takes up
residence inside someone else.

In my shed I was researching the Medusa myth and she had
taken up residence inside me. I wasn't too sure I liked her
being there. The Medusa was a woman who was both very
powerful and very upset. It was a peculiar myth about a
woman who returns the male gaze instead of looking away,
and it ends with her cruel beheading, the separating of the
head of a woman (the mind, subjectivity) from her body – as
if its potency is too threatening. Robert Graves speculated
that the reason for this decapitation was a bid to end the threat
of female power and assert male domination. To my surprise,
the Medusa had started to walk into my new novel.

At the time I was thinking about a woman who told me
that her husband never looked at her. 'Never. Even when he
speaks to me, he always looks somewhere else.' When I was
in their company I began to look at him never looking at her.
This woman who lived in a large house with her husband and
two fierce dogs (perhaps to guard them from risking a more
intimate exchange with each other) was being subjected to a
curious kind of passive violence. She began to take on more
responsibilities at work because she did not want to live
more hours in the day at home with him. They lived in

the same house but they lived separate lives and slept in separate bedrooms. When she returned home from her challenging professional life, she was pleased to have someone to watch films with in the evenings. But when they discussed the film afterwards, she said his eyes remained on the screen while he offered his opinions, long after the credits had stopped rolling. She wanted to leave the room and find somewhere else to be, but then she remembered she lived there and it was her home.

The moody politics of the modern home had become complicated and confusing. There were many modern and apparently powerful women I knew who had made a home for everyone else, but did not feel at home in their family home. They preferred the office or wherever they worked because they had more status than being a wife. Orwell, in his 1936 essay 'Shooting an Elephant', noted that the imperialist 'wears a mask, and his face grows to fit it'. The wife also wears a mask and her face grows to fit it, in all its variations. Some women who were the main earners in their family were being slyly punished by their men for any success they had achieved. Their male partners had become resentful, angry and depressed. As Simone de Beauvoir had told us, women are not supposed to eclipse men in a world in which success and power are marked out for them. It is not easy to take up the historic privilege of dominance over women (with a modern twist) if he is economically dependent on her talents. At the same time, she receives the fatal message that she must conceal her talents and abilities in order to be loved by him. They know they are both lying to save his face, which has also grown to fit the mask. His eyes stare through the peepholes, fearful the world will find him out. It is also the false head the caterpillar presents to predators. He knows the mask of the patriarchy is abnormal and perverse, but it is useful to protect him from being wounded. At its most decorated, the mask is there to help him appear to be rational while he intimidates women, children and other men. Above all, it is there to protect him from the anxiety of failure in the eyes of other men. If a man is considered successful because he succeeds in suppressing women (at home, at work, in bed) it would be a great achievement to be a failure in this regard.

The pain of the contemporary middle-aged male who, having failed to entirely suppress women, perceives himself as disempowered is a delicate matter. Their women lie delicately for them. Adrienne Rich has written a whole pithy chapter on the art of lying in her book *Arts of the Possible*. She points out that when we stop lying we create the possibility for more truth.

So, when I was next in the company of the man who never looked at his wife, I in turn began to look at him never looking at her – at the dining table for example, or in the car, or wherever it was he never looked at her. I wondered what his lack of looking was supposed to communicate. I had a go at trying to figure it out because the male gaze is supposed to work the other way – it is women who are looked at, we are not supposed to do the looking.

Perhaps he wanted to communicate his contempt for her: if I look at you, you will think that you exist for me. Or, if I look at you, you will see that I love you and I don't want to appear to be loving you. Or, in never looking at you, I am communicating my desire for you to never look at me in return. If you look at me too closely, you will see that I feel pathetic, ashamed and helpless.

It could have been all of these things. Probably the most complicated would be if he loved her, but did not want to appear to be loving her. That would be difficult to convey, but I had explored something similar through the avatar of Isabel, the wife and war correspondent in *Swimming Home*, who dares not love (or look at) the husband who continually betrays her. No, on balance, I thought he was clearly telling her that she did not exist for him. It was an odd twist on the Medusa myth, and other myths, too. His eyes, which he had plucked out like Oedipus, were staring at her anyway. All the time. He was trying to see her off. It was nothing less than attempted murder.

All writing is about looking and listening and paying attention to the world. Charlotte Brontë places this kind of looking at the heart of *Jane Eyre*. Just as the squirrels in the apple tree by my shed were aware that I was there all the time, Jane's cruel aunt, Mrs Reed, believes that her impoverished young niece is observing her all the time.

> . . . her incomprehensible disposition, and her sudden starts of temper, and her continual, unnatural watchings of one's movements!

That is how my mother felt about me.

NINE

NIGHT WANDERING

My mother taught me how to swim and she taught me how to row a boat. She was born in South Africa, grew up in 'the windy city' of Port Elizabeth and longed for the sea every day in the four decades she lived in North London. She always said that Doris Lessing's second novel, *Martha Quest*, forensically described her own life growing up in the sterility and ignorance of South Africa's white colonial culture. In old age my mother had found a swimming technique to 'totally give herself to the water'. This involved floating on her back, 'emptying her thoughts' and 'surrendering to the flow'. She showed me her trick in the murky swimming ponds on Hampstead Heath, floating Ophelia style with the ducks and weed and leaves.

I still try to do her trick, but I can only float for ten seconds before I start to sink. Likewise, when I turn my mind to my mother's death, I can only do so for ten seconds before I start to sink.

There is a photograph I have kept of my mother in her late twenties. She is sitting on a rock at a picnic with friends. Her hair is wet because she's just had a swim. There is a kind of introspection in her expression that I now relate to the very best of her. I can see that she is close to herself in this random moment. I'm not sure that I thought introspection was the best of her when I was a child and teenager. What do we need dreamy mothers for? We do not want mothers who gaze beyond us, longing to be elsewhere. We need her to be of this world, lively, capable, entirely present to our needs.

Did I mock the dreamer in my mother and then insult her for having no dreams?

As the vintage story goes, it is the father who is the hero and the dreamer. He detaches himself from the pitiful needs of his women and children and strides out into the world to do his thing. He is expected to be himself. When he returns to the home that our mothers have made for us, he is either welcomed back into the fold, or becomes a stranger who will eventually need us more than we need him. He tells us some of what he has seen in his world. We give him an edited version of the living we do every day. Our mothers live with us in this living and we blame her for everything because she is near by. At the same time, we try not to collude with myths about her character and purpose in life. All the same, we need her to feel anxiety on our behalf – after all, our everyday living is full of anxiety. If we do not disclose our feelings to her, we mysteriously expect her to understand them anyway. And if she moves beyond us, comes close to being a self that is not at our service, she has transgressed from the mythic, primal task of being our protector and nurturer. Yet, if she comes too close, she suffocates us, infecting our fragile courage with her contagious anxiety. When our father does the things he needs to do in the world, we understand it is his due. If our mother does the things she needs to do in the world, we feel she has abandoned us. It is a miracle she survives our mixed messages, written in society's most poisoned ink. It is enough to drive her mad.

I believe that always, or almost always, in all childhoods and in all the lives that follow them, the mother represents madness. Our mothers always remain the strangest, craziest people we've ever met.

– Marguerite Duras, *Practicalities*

When I was a teenager, most arguments with my mother were about clothes. She was baffled by what it was inside myself that I was expressing outside of myself. She could no longer reach or recognize me. And that was the whole point. I was creating a persona that was braver than I actually felt. I took the risk of being mocked on buses and in the streets of the suburbs in which I lived. The secret message that lurked in the zips of my silver platform boots was that I did not want to be like the people doing the mocking. Sometimes we want to unbelong as much as we want to belong. On a bad day, my mother would ask me, 'Who do you think you are?' I had no idea how to answer that question when I was fifteen, but I was reaching for the kind of freedom that a young woman in the 1970s did not socially possess. What else was there to do? To become the person someone else had imagined for us is not freedom – it is to mortgage our life to someone else's fear.

If we cannot at least imagine we are free, we are living a life that is wrong for us.

My mother was braver in her life than I have ever been. She escaped from the upper-class WASP family she loved and married a penniless Jewish historian. She became involved with him in the struggle for human rights in the South Africa of her generation. Clever, glamorous and witty, she never made it to university in her early twenties. No one thought it necessary to tell her she had an abundance of talent. Women of her class were expected to marry as soon as they left home, or after their first job. This was supposed to be a nominal job and not a serious career. My mother was taught to type, to learn shorthand and to wear clothes that pleased her male bosses. She wished she had been a less skilled secretary, but it was her fast typing that fed and clothed her children when my father became a political prisoner. She gave me a hard time, beyond the call of a dutiful daughter, but I can now see that I did not want to let her be herself, for better or worse.

A year after I moved with my daughters into the apartment on the hill, my mother became fatally sick. I lay awake all night waiting for a call from the hospital, each hour marked by the call of the various birds on my bird clock. The nightingale sang just before midnight, as if it were perched in the boughs of the dripping tree in the car park. She always said that when she died, she wanted her body to be carried to the peak of a mountain and then devoured by birds.

In the last few weeks of her dying, she was unable to eat or to drink water. However, I discovered that she was able to lick and swallow a particular brand of ice lolly. It came in three flavours – lime was her favourite, then strawberry, last of all the dreaded orange. Winter was not the best time for this particular ice lolly to be stocked in the shops, but I had found a supply of them in the freezer of my local newsagent, owned by three Turkish brothers. They often sold mushrooms in a box that was placed on the lid of this long, low freezer, which was positioned in the middle of the shop. Also placed on its lid were lottery tickets, reduced-price cleaning products, cans of fizzy drinks, shoe polish, batteries and pastries. Inside this freezer were the ice lollies that were my mother's only comfort during her dying. At the time I was so devastated from my shipwrecked marriage and my mother's diagnosis of cancer, both happening within a year of each other, I was unable to explain to the brothers why I bought ice lollies every day in February. I arrived grim-faced, eyes always wet, my bicycle parked outside. Without saying a single word, I began to move the mushrooms, lottery tickets, reduced-price cleaning products, cans of fizzy drinks, shoe polish, batteries and pastries to one side of the freezer. Then I'd slide the door open and search for the lollies – triumphant when I found the lime, good if I found strawberry, acceptable when I found the orange. I'd always buy two and then cycle to the hospital down the hill where my mother was dying.

I would sit by her bed and hold the ice lolly to her lips, pleased to hear her ooh and aah with pleasure. She was always insatiably thirsty. There was a fridge in her room but not a freezer, so the second lolly would melt, but my ritual was to always buy two. Looking back on this, I don't know why I didn't buy all the lollies in the newsagent and put them in my own freezer, but somehow it never occurred to me at this difficult time. And then one day, a terrible thing happened in the lolly scheme of things. As usual, I cycled to the newsagent, whooshed everything that was resting on the lid of the freezer aside, and, watched by the baffled Turkish brothers, slid open the freezer door. It turned out there was a fourth flavour. The brothers had run out of lime, strawberry and even the dreaded orange. I looked up from the freezer, straight into the kind brown eyes of the youngest brother.

'Why have you only got bubblegum flavour?' I started to shout – why would anyone bother to make a bubblegum ice lolly, never mind sell it? What was the point and could they urgently stock up on the other flavours, particularly the lime?

The brother did not shout back. He just stood in baffled silence while I angrily purchased two bubblegum-flavoured lollies. It felt like a catastrophe as I cycled to the hospital, and actually it was a catastrophe because they were more or less the only things keeping her alive for another day.

I tried a few other shops on the way to the hospital, but none of them stocked the brand that was easy to swallow. So I sat by my skeletal mother's bed, unwrapped the bubblegum ice lolly and moved it to her lips. She licked it, grimaced, tried it again and then shook her head. When I told her how I had raved and ranted like a lunatic in the shop, these tiny sounds came out of her mouth, her chest moving up and down. I knew she was laughing and it is one of my favourite memories of our last days together. That night when I was reading a book by her bed, I glanced in remorse at the bubblegum lolly melting into a pink blob in the basin. I wasn't really reading, just skimming the page, but it was comforting to be near her. When the doctor came into the room to do her last rounds, my mother lifted her thin hand and somehow managed to make the tiny voice she had at this time sound imperious and commanding: 'Arrange for some light. My daughter is reading in the dark.'

After her funeral in March, I thought I should go back to the newsagent and explain my weird behaviour to the Turkish brothers. When I told them about the last weeks of my mother's life they were so upset it was their turn not to speak. They shook their heads and sighed and groaned. After a while, the oldest brother said, 'If only you had told us.' The brother who wore fashionable jackets picked up the conversation, 'If you had said something we would have gone to the cash and carry and bought a ton for you,' while the third brother, whose voice was higher pitched than his older brothers, thumped his hand to his forehead, 'I knew it was something like that . . . didn't I say she was buying them for someone who was sick?' They all looked angrily at the freezer, as if it was personally responsible for the horror of the bubblegum lolly being the wrong sort of lolly in the last few days of my mother's life. This time I laughed, which gave them permission to laugh, too. It was a big release from the terror of death to finally acknowledge that it is also always absurd. We were standing on the flattened cardboard boxes laid on the floor to protect the lino from the muddy feet of customers. It was soggy and stained and slid beneath our feet as we laughed. I felt much better after I had explained things to the Turkish brothers, and in a way, I wish I had explained things more to the father of my children.

When I returned to the newsagent one Sunday to buy some of the mushrooms I had spent weeks angrily flinging to the other end of the freezer lid, the youngest brother had just returned from his vacation in Turkey. He handed me an object wrapped in newspaper and told me it was a gift. It turned out to be a tiny white china cup that slid into a latticed silver holder, with an ornate silver lid that fitted over the cup. He said he remembered how when I bought a packet of Turkish coffee from the shop, I had told him I drank it in a glass. 'But a glass is for tea,' he said, 'so this is the right sort of cup for Turkish coffee.'

I understood that it was a gift of condolence.

To this day, that cup marks my mother leaving the world. I have yet to tell him that sometimes when I write, I make Turkish coffee in a small copper pot, pour it into this very cup and then slip the silver lid over the top. It has become part of my writing ritual. To sip strong aromatic coffee from midnight to the small hours always brings something interesting to the page. I have become a night wanderer without moving from my writing chair. The night is softer than the day, quieter, sadder, calmer, the sound of the wind tapping windows, the hissing of pipes, the entropy that makes floorboards creak, the ghostly night bus that comes and goes – and always in cities, a far-off distant sound that resembles the sea, yet is just life, *more life*. I realized that was what I wanted after my mother's death. More life.

I somehow thought she would die and still be alive. I would like to think she is somewhere in that distant sound that resembles the sea in which she taught me to swim, but she is not there. She has gone, slipped away, disappeared.

A few months after her death I was reading from *Things I Don't Want to Know* at a festival in Berlin. The translator sat at my side. We had agreed that I would read three lines in English and she would translate those three lines into German for the audience. I started to read, and then I came to a section in which I am seven years old, lying in my mother's arms. It was a shock I had not anticipated, a ghostly encounter.

Our heads touched. It was love and it was pain.

My voice broke and I paused mid-sentence. The translator waited for me to finish the agreed three sentences. She was left stranded, a broken sentence hanging between us. If the words were trains they had slowed right down and then come to a halt. When they eventually pulled into the station, splattered with the dust of the African past, the translator's tone was clipped and matter-of-fact – which might have been a good thing. This struggle to get the words out of my mouth took me right back to a year in my childhood when I did not speak at all. Every time I was asked to speak up, to speak louder, the words ran away, trembling and ashamed. It is always the struggle to find language that tells me it is alive, vital, of great importance. We are told from an early age that it is a good thing to be able to express ourselves, but there is as much invested in putting a stop to language as there is in finding it. Truth is not always the most entertaining guest at the dinner table, and anyway, as Duras suggests, we are always more unreal to ourselves than other people are.

After my reading in Berlin, I was sitting with my German publisher outside the authors' tent. She had a question to ask me.

'When you read out loud, are you an actress?'

She was referring to the highly emotional way those lines had at last been delivered to the audience. This was my opportunity to explain to her that my mother had recently died and how it was a shock to re-find her on the pages of my book. But I did not say that. I said nothing at all. So the Turkish brothers fared better than my publisher.

'You look very pale,' she said. I did not know how to reply to that either.

After a while, I pointed to a vendor in the festival grounds selling currywurst, and told her that I wanted to write about a character, a major male character, who would stand by a currywurst wagon in the snow of Berlin, waiting for someone he had betrayed.

'Currywurst is not a romantic dish,' she interrupted me.

'Yes,' I replied, 'but love is like war; it always finds a way.'

Love did find its way through the on-and-off war between myself and my mother. The poet Audre Lorde said it best: 'I am a reflection of my mother's secret poetry as well as of her hidden angers.' She sent me a postcard from Johannesburg in 1992, where she had travelled to see the friends who had helped support her family in the years of political turmoil, the transition from apartheid to democracy.

Kicked off hols to a glorious start by going to Walter Sisulu's birthday celebrations. Saw people not seen for

what seems a 100 years. Sat next to Nadine Gordimer.
She is tiny & thin & bird-like & bright.

My mother had made a biro'd X on the front of the postcard and written, *X is where I am.* She seems to have been located in a neighbourhood somewhere beyond a big flyover, near a telephone tower and skyscraper. It is this X that touches me most now, her hand holding the biro, pressing it into the postcard, marking where she is so that I can find her.

TEN

X IS WHERE I AM

I lost all sense of geographical direction for a few weeks after my mother's death. I was disorientated, as if some sort of internal navigation system was drifting. At this time of mourning, I did not want to ride my e-bike and had downloaded an app for a cab firm on my smartphone. The driver was then routed to my pickup location, the idea being that he would drive me to my destination with the help of satnav. This is when I experienced the primal terror of being lost in my own beloved London, yet in the hands of a driver who did not have a clue where he was going. I could say that satnav was not a reliable mother.

Where are we now? Where were we before?

These were not questions the driver could answer. There was no X in his mind's eye. If the satnav directed him south when I was heading north, that's what we were going to do.

Satnav was his only compass. We were driving at the beginning of Genesis when the earth was formless and empty – apart from the signs on the screen. It seemed to me that satnav had switched off the way that drivers inhabited a city. It made them rootless, ahistorical, unable to trust their memory or senses, to measure the distance between one place and another. The River Thames, referred to by Londoners as *the river*, was of no geographical significance to the driver. Its brackish water, mostly salt water, flowing for 215 miles, was just one of many abstract rivers flowing through the abstract cities of the world. *The river*, once the Port of London where apprentices ate salmon fished from its depths, was now just a grammar of digital signs. As I listened to the calm but firm robot voice giving directions, I realized we could be anywhere, so long as the Voice was with us. There were no *landmarks*. The driver did not look at the Albert Hall when we passed it on the northern edge of South Kensington, he was absent to its physical presence, and instead was existentially *alone but together* with his satnav. The Albert Hall in Old English was a *landmearc*, but he worked with digital *mearcs* – with the bonus of live traffic updates.

Perhaps this time of vertigo was so extreme because I had been severed from my own origins. My mother was my link to Africa and to England. Her body was my first *landmearc*. It was she who had raised her children and most childhood memories were twinned with her presence on earth. She was my primal satnav, but now the screen had gone blank.

If we were driving through an ancient city guided by a digital Voice, I too was immersed in the handheld devices I carried with me. They had become, in the words of the writer Sherry Turkle, my *second self*, as I searched for passwords I had forgotten or for something on Google – so many questions to ask, after all.

How do you register a death?

At this time, I became a magnet for other people who were lost in all kinds of ways. I took a ride in a London black cab where the driver absolutely knew the way around his city, but his mind was lost, shattered. His conversation was crazy. He told me he was looking for cashpoints in London, holes in the walls, so that he could communicate with aliens who were waiting for his message. I decided to jump out of his cab before we reached our destination. On balance I preferred the saner drivers who were humbly clueless.

The man who cried at the funeral told me that he also lost his sense of direction after his long-time lover had died. He had a week's leave off work and offered to be my chauffeur.

He advised me to take advantage of his time and suggested that I should also take a week off work. I told him I couldn't afford it, but in the end I gave in. He more or less knew where he was going. Sometimes his new lover, Geoff, would come along for the ride. Another time, there was a stranger sitting in the car. It was the woman with the long black hair, Clara, who had been sitting on a red velvet sofa at the party. She was his colleague, an academic from South America who was on leave in the UK on a research fellowship. I wasn't sure why Clara was in the car with us, but she seemed to enjoy the ride. When we were stuck in traffic, she took out her pen and started to write something on a slip of paper. She looked slightly tormented, as if she was attempting to untangle a difficult thought, so I looked over her shoulder to see what she was writing.

tomatoes avocados ~~lemons~~ limes

One day when we were driving down the three kilometres of the Holloway Road, I said to her, 'This is the Holloway Road. It's a bit like the Adriatic Sea.' Clara stared out of the window at the three lanes of traffic. A police car, its siren switched on, was speeding through the bus lane. Beer cans, broken umbrellas and a takeaway carton of discarded chips lay in a heap on the pavement. Clara asked for the English word that

described the surface of the road. Geoff, who wore his spec-
tacles on a chain around his neck, lifted them up to his eyes
and peered through the lens as if he was at the opera. He
asked her if she meant *tarmac*?

'Yes,' she replied, 'under the tarmac, the beach.'

It was like having a holiday in a car with three interesting
companions.

The man who cried at the funeral told me that Clara was a
distinguished professor and that his students did not turn up
on time to her lectures, they arrived *early*. She was researching
popular uprisings against military and bureaucratic elites. It
turned out that Clara liked to swim every day. We agreed that
we could swim together, but only if we did not speak to each
other in the water. We were dropped off at various pools
around London and discovered that we had lots to talk about
in-between lengths of front crawl. She plaited her hair when
she swam. When she lost her turquoise ring in the water she
asked the lifeguard to drain the pool. He thought she was
joking but she meant it. In the end we found her ring by the
side of the pool where she had left it tucked inside her book.
Our chauffeur was always there to pick us up afterwards,
damp towels rolled under our arms. We went to pubs for lunch
and walked in London parks. It was spring and daffodils were

pushing through the grass. In a way, having a chauffeur was like having a parent, but without the history.

Clara offered to cook a meal at my flat. I accepted on the condition that my temporary chauffeur and his now permanent lover joined the table. She went off to buy a fish called tilapia but came back with red snappers. I had been instructed to buy limes (not lemons), avocados, tomatoes. She confessed that the communal corridors in the building scared the life out of her.

'Yes', I said, 'I call them The Corridors of Love.'

She began to fry the fish and the kitchen filled with smoke. She was serene and good company. She had also brought with her a bottle of aguardiente, a strong liqueur flavoured with aniseed. She reckoned her firewater was good for bereavement. 'It is very numbing.'

She told me about her city, her politics and her family. She asked me questions: where, when, where? I told her the first nine years of myself were made in southern Africa; I had made the rest in Britain. While she squeezed limes on to the red snappers, she wondered if I was nostalgic for my childhood in Africa? I told her that I regarded nostalgia as a waste of time. I have never wanted to cover the past in dust sheets to preserve it from change. She told me that the seeds of the future are always planted in the past. Apparently the limes I had bought were the wrong sort of limes. She kept asking me questions. In my long marriage it was a relief to never be asked questions. At the time that suited me very well. There was so much I did not want to talk about.

Clara cooked and asked for utensil directions – 'Where are your spoons, where is the breadboard, why is there a butterfly in your kitchen?' I told her it was a moth. We talked about Sundays, dim sum, guava jelly, money, siblings, mosquitoes, the good and bad things about our middle years – which we decided were mostly good. We talked about her research and about my shed, and how Celia was currently reading a book of poems by the Welsh writer Alun Lewis, titled *Ha! Ha! Among the Trumpets*. When Celia was fifteen she had found this book in the school library. She was now reading it out loud to me in her kitchen, age eighty-four. Clara thought my life was *la dolce vita*.

Yes and No, I replied. 'Why Yes and No?' I could barely see her through the smoke. The red fish had now turned black. I explained to her some of what lay between Yes and No. While she chopped an onion with a butter knife, she said, 'You should open the front door for our friends. Do you know there's something wrong with your bell?' When I returned to the kitchen, she was frying onions and chilli in a separate pan from the fish.

I reached through the smoke to pass her the salt.

Clara said, 'Can I take a photo of you on my phone?'

'Okay, but you can't see anything because of the smoke. By the way, there's a sharper knife in the drawer.'

Flash.

She slipped her phone into the back pocket of her jeans and asked if I ever put sea salt in my bath, 'It makes the water softer.' She had noticed that the London water coming out of the taps in my sink was hard water. 'By the way,' she said, 'the professors at my university here in London tend to watch cricket. Do you like the game?'

I told her I prefer fencing. She scooped up a strand of her long black hair that had come undone and whisked it over her shoulder, away from the high flame on the hob. She told me that she and her brothers used to fight each other with sticks, which was similar to fencing. I had to understand that she was her father's only daughter because she had seven brothers. It was hard to find a quiet place to study. There were times she did her homework inside the cupboard under the stairs. Her mother had cooked for her family of ten and then sat alone in the kitchen to eat one small bowl of rice. She suddenly jumped away from the frying pan and asked if there was a bird in my house. I explained she had just heard the woodpecker making its call inside my bird clock.

'You should get rid of those idiot birds,' she said.

'It's funny you say that,' I replied, 'because that's what I said to one of my writing students.'

'Why do you like the bird clock, anyway?'

I thought about this for a while.

'The birds keep me company and interrupt sad thoughts.'

'Yes, I understand.' She looked quite professorial at that moment, even with a wooden spoon in her hand.

'You know,' she said, 'my mother liked to eat alone in the kitchen because it was the only place she could hear herself think. She had no other place to go. But you have a shed to hear yourself think. Do you have a bird clock in your shed?'

I told her I did not.

'My mother's purpose in life was for birthing. She lived for her man and for her children. She did not think that was the worst life she could have. She was not a private person. She was a public person. Everyone in the neighbourhood consulted my mother.'

She told me my daughters would like the local white cheese from where she was from. It was mild and fresh.

'So,' she said, 'can you see yourself living with someone again?'

'At a distance,' I replied. 'Long distance.'

'No,' she said, 'too much happens between departing and arriving to live long distance. The cells in the body change between the space of departing and arriving.'

I asked her to tell me about her turquoise ring.

She chose not to do so.

'What are those?' She pointed to my daughters' childhood fishing nets, which were tucked into the broom cupboard.

I still could not talk about those nets, so I did not reply. They were portals to the past, like flowers, like everything, perhaps like a turquoise ring.

She yanked one of the nets out and inspected it.

'The cane is too long. It should be shorter so you can move more swiftly to catch the fish.'

At that moment the man who cried at the funeral walked into the smoke with his lover.

'We are shortening the past,' Clara said, pointing to the fishing net, 'but really it is a reactionary desire to silence knowledge.'

ELEVEN

FOOTSTEPS IN THE HOUSE

Where are we now? Where were we before?

I was at St Pancras International station on the Euston Road, waiting to take the Eurostar to Paris for the French publication of *Swimming Home*. Apparently I had to arrive at the Gare du Nord in time for a *breakfast* interview. It was 4am and I was gazing at the departure screens, a paper cup of coffee in my hand. Further into the station was a bronze statue of a man and woman entwined in an amorous embrace. Were they arriving or departing?

I was surrounded by all the sounds and signals of travel – people wheeling their suitcases, the last-minute search for various documents, the buying of bottles of water and newspapers. As I listened to announcements of cancellations and arrivals, what came to mind, out of the blue and into the orange London dawn, was the train that my family had boarded just after we arrived at Southampton docks from South Africa in 1968. This train was going to take us to Waterloo station. I had been sitting next to my brother, and in the aisle seats opposite us were our mother and father. We were all looking out of the window at ENGLAND.

I had always told myself that this was a happy train ride. Yes, the story I had told myself was that we were laughing and chatting and eating crisps. I realized that morning at St Pancras International that the train ride to Waterloo had been a terrifying journey. I was nine years old. Where were our things? Where were my clothes? My toys? Where was our stuff? The furniture from our family home? Where were we going to live in England, anyway? Would I go to school somewhere? We had not been chatting and laughing at all. I had anxiously read the name of every station on the way to Waterloo. My mother's hands were shaking when she showed the conductor our rail tickets. My father was looking out of the window. My mother was looking at her children.

That is where I was before.

By the time I found my carriage and boarded the Eurostar, the newly retrieved sound of my silent, shaken family on that train from Southampton docks was still queasily lingering in my ears. It had taken a long time to *hear* it. Even longer to *feel* it. The Eurostar passengers, like myself, were all half asleep. The men had shaved, some of the women wore full make-up. We found our seats, took off our coats, laid our laptops and tablets and smartphones on the tables. The train pulled out of St Pancras, and began its journey towards France, which would take just over two hours.

A young woman sat next to me, perhaps seventeen, her hair dyed blue. She was wired up with earphones attached to her laptop, learning French from a basic language program. It required her to say out loud the words being spoken by a robot voice speaking French. She obviously could not say the words out loud in our carriage, but her lips, which were pierced with a tiny silver ring, were moving as she whispered verbs and nouns. I glanced at her screen on our shared table and saw a note that told her French has two grammatical genders, masculine and feminine; a woman was feminine, but so was a chair, while hair was masculine.

She had plaited her own blue hair for the journey, two plaits, the ends tied with bands sewn with tiny pink cotton rosebuds. It was very expressed hair. She had told me that she was from Devon, and when I asked where in Devon, she said, 'The countryside.'

When the Eurostar arrived at Ashford International, the last stop before we went through the tunnel under the sea, a man in his early seventies sat on the seat opposite us. He asked the teenager if she'd mind moving her computer so that he had more space at the table. She moved it to her lap. This was a small rearrangement of space, but its outcome meant she had entirely removed herself from the table to make space for his newspaper, sandwich and apple.

After a while, he told me he was travelling to Paris to pick up the pair of shoes that his wife had left in their hotel room. Apparently, they had recently spent a weekend in Paris for their wedding anniversary. His wife had told him not to bother to make the journey to retrieve the shoes, but he said he had no choice because he did not trust the post to deliver them safely to their house on the North Downs in Kent. When he lifted the apple to his lips and bit into it, I leaned over to the young woman and said, 'That apple is feminine . . . in French.'

'*La pomme*,' she said, frowning, but what she actually said was, '*La pomme?*', as if she wasn't too sure that was right, which is why she was frowning.

Meanwhile the man was telling me he certainly did not relish the return journey back from Paris. 'You know,' he whispered, 'migrants and refugees break into the tunnel and climb on to the roof of these trains.' He pointed to his right ear. 'You have to be vigilant and listen for the sound of footsteps.'

'Will you do that?' I asked him. 'Will you listen for the sound of footsteps on the roof of the train?'

'Oh yes,' he said, 'I will *hear* them.'

I asked him if the shoes his wife had left in Paris were special? After all, he was travelling all the way to Paris to collect them.

By this time the blue-haired woman had removed the headphones from her ears, partly because it was too uncomfortable to concentrate on her language program with the computer on her lap.

He told us both that his wife's shoes were medical shoes. His wife had one leg shorter than the other and so she wore a raised left shoe. This shoe had a heel built into it and had been made to help correct her balance and align her spine.

I wanted to ask him what sort of shoes his wife (no name) had been wearing for the return journey from Paris to Kent. If she had left these vital shoes in their hotel room, did she have a spare pair of medical shoes? It felt intrusive to ask him to elaborate on his wife's feet, but he did volunteer that 'without these particular medical shoes, he could not hear her footsteps in the house'. Usually, he knew if she was making her way to the bathroom or if she was walking down the stairs, because the left shoe made a tapping sound on the floor. Now that she was wearing lighter shoes it was hard for him to follow her movement, which, he said, 'was a bit nerve-racking'.

I asked if he was nervous that she would fall?

No, her balance was stable. In fact the lighter shoes were her preference but he felt urgently compelled to retrieve the medical shoes from Paris so he could hear her footsteps in the house.

He seemed obsessed with footsteps. I wondered if his wife had chosen to leave her shoes in Paris to avoid her husband knowing where she was at all times. Certainly, if there were migrants clinging to the roof of the train, they too were making a bid to slip away. It would seem that he had given himself the job of making sure that no one slipped away on his watch.

Now that he had finished his apple, I suggested to the young woman that she put her laptop back on the table. She did so, but at an odd angle in order to make space for the man's newspaper, which he had placed in the middle of the table. When I asked him to move the newspaper to make room for her laptop, he asked me to repeat my request twice, as if he had no comprehension of the way I was using the English language. In the end I said, 'She's studying,' and when he did not understand that either, I said, 'She's working.'

An announcement was made in English and then in French to tell us we were about to enter the tunnel. There was more information in two languages. We would be travelling under the sea for twenty-four miles and it would take fourteen minutes.

In we go. We are travelling through what was once an ocean of chaos and darkness. Low tides. High tides. Plankton. Coral. We are 150 feet under the seabed.

The Eurostar was really a submarine. I closed my eyes and drifted into a light sleep that was haunted with footsteps. First the *tap tap* of the raised medical shoes that shackled the unnamed wife. These footsteps became softer in the general whooshing thick sound of the tunnel under the sea, softer,

softer, barely there, but I heard footsteps all the same. Were migrants walking on the roof of the train? No. It was the sound of bare feet on *tarmac*. Who do the footsteps belong to? Do footsteps *belong* to someone? Yes, they belong to *her*.

She is nine years old and she is crossing the tarmac of the Holloway Road.

Her mother, who is now dead, has cut her fringe crooked with nail scissors. She is myself and she is walking in the rain towards my family house, towards my old life. My married life. The address is written on her arm, which is still tanned, although she has lived in England for two months. She is wearing a summer dress and she is barefoot. She has stopped obediently at the red robot, which she has learned is called a *traffic light* in England, just as tomato sauce is called *ketchup*, and a potato chip is a *crisp*. She asks for directions and her accent is strange. People are kind. She smiles all the time, she is charming and pretty. Her eyes are green, her eyebrows are black. There are enough kind people around to point her in the right direction. A few of them are surprised she is not wearing shoes, but she never wears shoes if she can get away with it. She finds the street just off the Holloway Road near Whittington Park. She is looking for the Victorian house where her middle-aged self, now in her forties, has made a home for her family.

When she knocks on the door of the Victorian semi, a woman shouts, *Who are you?* Her accent is English, her voice is deep.

I am you, the girl shouts back in a thick South African accent.

The rain continues to fall on the child stranded outside the door of her assimilated more or less English older self, who is cowering on the other side of the door. What will happen if she invites this nine-year-old into the house with its Victorian plumbing and her English daughters, one age twelve, the other six, both of them watching *The Great British Bake Off* on the TV in the living room?

The foreign girl is stubborn and won't go away. She smells of another place. Of plants that have grown in the African soil, the hot cement pavements after a rainstorm, of peeling the rough skin off lychees. She has sunshine in the tips of her hair, she has only swum in oceans in which nets have been laid out to deter sharks, she has cried at the sight of the postbox where she posted letters to her father. During the four years he was a political prisoner in the struggle for democracy in southern

Africa, she was practically mute for a year of her life, but now she is boldly hammering at the door. When it eventually opens, she steps in. Her wet, bare feet make a trail in the corridor. She turns left into the living room and jumps on to the sofa with the English children. These are the daughters she will give birth to in her thirties.

Mary Berry tastes a sponge cake. Paul Hollywood is breaking a slice apart with his big hands to test it is moist and feather-light. It seems the South African child is happy to concentrate on the pleasures of baking. Her middle-aged self watches this child warily. She does not want her to make trouble for her daughters and tell them to get some real problems when they complain about not having the right brand of trainers for school. She has never wanted her own children to have to be brave. Brave like the children on leaking boats fleeing wars. How many medals does a child need pinned on to her pyjamas? Nothing had taught her that having to summon an abundance of courage, far more than anyone should have to bear, is healthy for a child. She had witnessed the courage of the African children in her country of birth who lost their parents in the struggle for human rights like other children lost their milk teeth.

She watches her nine-year-old self agree with the English kids that the cake on the left is the best because the jam is evenly distributed and it's not too sweet and she cheers when the judges agree with her. She is pleased the foreign girl seems to feel at home in her home. To make a family home needs time, dedication and, above all, empathy. To be hospitable to strangers is the point of having a home, although this child is not exactly a stranger.

And then they all turn their heads. A man has walked into the room with a beer in his right hand. The child who is not exactly a stranger does not know this is the English man she will marry twenty-five years later. He can't see her either. He will meet her in Cambridge, where she will be living in a set of rooms opposite Wittgenstein's rooms.

You get tragedy when the tree, instead of bending, breaks.

They will live with each other for over two decades in this house. And then their marriage, instead of bending, will break. They will pack up all the baking tins and take the clock off the kitchen wall.

At the Gare du Nord my editor met me at the gates and escorted me to the breakfast interview. The first question I

was asked was the meaning of these lines, which I wrote in
that house off the Holloway Road.

> Life is only worth living because we hope it will get better
> and we'll all get home safely.

TWELVE

THE BEGINNING OF EVERYTHING

My best male friend was now married for the third time. He had insisted on buying the yellow jacket to wear at his wedding and I now referred to it as his Yellow Wallpaper. In the book of the same title by Charlotte Perkins Gilman, a wife tries to escape from her husband and from her life through the yellow wallpaper of the family home.

One night my best male friend arrived, uninvited, at my flat at eleven in the evening wearing this jacket, which peculiarly still had the safety pin that had attached the wedding nosegay of blue cornflowers to its lapel. He did not seem to want to go home. At around midnight we were standing on the balcony of my crumbling apartment block on the hill when we saw something flying towards us through the sky. At first we could not work out what it was, but then we saw it was not one thing but three things. They were birds. When they landed on the railings of the balcony, he started to cough, quite a hacking cough, but it did not seem to frighten them. The birds had turned their heads to the side, as if they were looking elsewhere, but we knew they were gazing at us. When we leaned in closer to look at their crest feathers, we thought they might be parrots. They did not like being stared at so bluntly, in fact this seemed to disturb them more than the sound of his hacking cough. The thinnest bird began to tug and pull at its feathers, which made us uneasy, so we decided to go back inside and look them up on the Internet.

As I took out my laptop we confessed that when we first saw the birds heading towards us, our minds had gone all over the place. We thought they might be drones or even missiles. I opened my laptop and started to google the parrots. He sat next to me, elbows on the table, pouring more wine, our eyes on the screen.

'You know,' I said, 'this year has been full of birds. I don't know what's going on. It all started with my bird clock.'

Apparently there were colonies of feral parrots living wild in London. We decided that the birds looked more like cockatoos. They liked to eat small lizards, seeds, fruit, roots and vegetables.

We returned to the balcony to have another look at them. The bird at the end of the line, the thin one that had been pulling out its feathers, had now changed places with the plumper bird in the middle. The yellow feathers on their wings sort of matched the photograph of the cockatoos we'd just studied on the screen. We thought we should feed them, so we cut up an apple and a banana and laid the fruit on the small round table positioned under the railings. They did not seem interested so we turned our backs on them and walked inside to finish off the bottle of wine.

He raised his glass. 'Here's to knowing each other all these years and to our long friendship.'

I clinked my glass with his glass.

'To when we were fifteen and immortal,' he continued. 'And to our poor parents who we made so anxious all the time. And to recovering from the knocks of the past few years. We are no longer merely grazed. In fact we are *hurt*.'

His phone was pinging.

'That will be Nadia,' I said.

'No, it's not my wife,' he insisted. 'It's a robot selling me insurance. Nadia doesn't care where I am. I bore Nadia, nothing I say interests her. She apparently knows what I am about to say and resents having to live through the time of me saying it. In fact she can barely look at me, she's got a lot on and she seems to be repulsed by my body as well.'

'You should go home,' I said.

'No,' he was shouting now, 'you're not listening. I no longer feel welcome in my own home.'

'I'm sorry to hear that.'

'No, no, you don't understand,' his fingers tore at what was left of his hair, ' "I love her and that is the beginning of every-thing." '

He told me that was a quote from F. Scott Fitzgerald.

'I am not really that great a person, but I'm not the worst catch either. Do you agree?'

I said that I did agree. And that as far as I was concerned he was a major character in my life.

'How do you mean, *character*? I'm not a *character*.'

I told him about how I had been asked to make a list of minor and major characters by the film executives.

'Actually,' I said, 'you are a minor major character.'

'What? I've been demoted?'

'Yes.'

I could see him and Nadia in a parody of a Jean-Luc Godard movie, both of them whispering in a café next to a train station, taking it in turns to convey to the camera (in fragmented voice-over) how it was all so impossible and how their failure to communicate their love only deepened their solitude and how they felt crushed by each other's contempt.

I'm unhappy with you and I'm unhappy alone.

The problem from a scriptwriter's point of view was that he could never be a major Godard character because his teeth were too white and he wasn't reflective enough to deliver a long internal monologue.

'I'm not that clever, it's true,' he said. 'Nadia finds me intellectually deficient as well. She's much cleverer than I am. But any way,' he reached for my hand and kissed it like an old-fashioned gigolo, 'I don't want to rub salt into the wound, but being alone doesn't suit you nearly as much as you think it does.'

I made Turkish coffee and poured it into two small cups.

Was it true that being alone did not suit me? In my old life I sometimes felt unreal to myself. What did *unreal* mean?

If I ever felt free enough to write my life as I felt it, would the point be to feel *more* real? What was it that I was reaching for? Not for *more* reality, that was for sure. I certainly did not want to write the major female character that has always been written for *Her.* I was more interested in a major unwritten female character.

We could hear the birds through the walls when his phone pinged again.

This time he reckoned it was his Uber receipt coming through.

'You came here in an Uber?'

'Yes.'

'Why don't you go home in an Uber?'

'I'll call a minicab.'

He took off his yellow jacket and lay flat out on his back on the floor, hands behind his neck, staring at the ceiling. I lay on the sofa, kicked off my shoes and stretched out my legs. It was convivial to laze around with someone at the end of the day. To not have to speak or ask each other to take out the garbage or mend something that was broken or to discuss our children (though we often did) and to know that we truly wished the best for each other – and not the worst. I must have dozed off, because I was woken by something fluttering against my cheek. At first I thought the birds had flown inside, but it was just a loose thread from the sofa. The doorbell, which was now fixed, was ringing. It turned out to be Nadia, tall and majestic, wrapped in a heavy winter coat.

'Is he here?'

'Yes.'

'It's four o'clock in the morning,' she said. 'He is supposed to be picking up my father from Heathrow at eight.'

I showed her in and she glanced at her husband, who was asleep on the floor. She tapped his stomach with the toe of her boot and prodded the leather hard into his stomach until he opened his eyes.

'Hello Nadia.' He reached out his arms so she could help pull him up from the floor. She did not take up his invitation and he was left stranded with his arms outstretched, while her hands remained in the pockets of her big winter coat.

The image stayed with me for a long time.

I invited her to look at the birds.

The loudest cockatoo was circling a chunk of bruised apple it had found on the table. Nadia wanted to know where they came from.

I told her I didn't know. They had arrived just after midnight in a pack of three.

Nadia raised her eyes towards the sky and shuddered, as if it was hiding in its grey infinity any number of exotic winged creatures waiting to land.

'Look at the fog,' she said, 'where has it come from? The flights into Heathrow might be delayed. *He* can drive and I'll sleep on the back seat until we get to Terminal 3.'

When they left they were still not really speaking to each other, but I thought they were in love all the same. I drank a glass of cool water and then I poured some of the water into a small bowl for the birds and carried it to the balcony. The fog had not yet lifted, but I could see the plump cockatoo perched in the middle of the line. It had raised its crested head and was shaking itself from the core of its being. A fine white powder rose from the depths of its feathers and fell like salt at its feet.

THIRTEEN

THE MILKY WAY

I talk to my mother for the first time since her death. She is listening. I am listening. That makes a change. I tell her I am writing a novel about a mother and daughter. There is a long silence. How are you, mother of mine, wherever you are? I hope there are owls close by. You always loved owls. Do you know that a few days after your death, when I was browsing in a department store on Oxford Street, I saw a pair of owl earrings with green glass eyes. I was suddenly flooded with inexplicable happiness. *I'll buy these earrings for my mother.*

I carried them to the counter to pay, but as the shop assistant took them from my hand, I realized you were dead.

Oh No No No No

When I uttered these words out loud, I sounded mad and tragic, as if I was from some other century altogether. I walked away, leaving the little jewelled owls in her hands. At that moment, I came too close to understanding the way Hamlet speaks Shakespeare's most sorrowful words. I mean, not just the actual words, but how he might sound when he says them.

They do not sound pretty, that's for sure. I couldn't get out of that shop fast enough.

Oh No No No No

Sorrow does not have a century.

I began to wonder for the first time how it was that Shakespeare's pen had moved the lips of Hamlet to open and close and open again to speak the struggling words that so accurately described the way my mind could not accept your death. And then I read that he wrote *Hamlet* in the year his father died. The line that means the most to me in the entire play is Hamlet's reply when asked what it is he is reading.

Words, words, words.

I think he is trying to say that he is inconsolable.
Words can cover up everything that matters.
I don't see ghosts but I can *hear* you listening.
The war is over for you.

Here's some news from the living. I have been visited by birds all this year, in one way or another. Some of them are real and some of them are less real.

But your owls are true. I have stopped thinking about why I am obsessed with birds, but it might be something to do with death and renewal. In the autumn, I made a new garden in the bathroom. The tall cactus had been on its way out for a long time, then it shrivelled and turned brown. I stood in the bath and heaved it off the shelf. I kept the smaller silver cactus but this time I potted jasmine and lilies and ferns. Do you know that jasmine, like orange blossom, has a scent that is otherworldly but it can sometimes smell like drains? The fern hangs over the bath; the lilies make their adjustments to the light. The small silver cactus with its arms pointing towards the ceiling looks like it is praying for rain.

And so am I. Every day is hard.

And I love the rain.

Thank you for teaching me how to swim and how to row a boat. Thank you for the typing jobs that put food in the fridge. As for myself, I have things to do in the world and have to get on with them and be more ruthless than you were.

FOURTEEN

GOOD TIDINGS

I met with the father of my children to discuss Christmas Day. It was the second Christmas since we had separated, though we had walked side by side, together but apart, for many years. We talked about the menu and who would cook what on the day, and shared ideas for our daughters' presents. We were in a chain coffee bar, sitting on brown leather armchairs facing each other. A Joni Mitchell song was playing through the speakers. It was about hating and loving someone, but we pretended not to notice.

We discussed the news and talked about the weather. Not once did we mention the tempest that had sunk the boat. We were both still angry with each other, but we were calm and I was certainly bewildered by how I never found him boring.

It was as if we had made a pact, from the moment we met, to know less about each other rather than more. I accepted this was the fatal flaw that tore us apart, and hoped that we would do better in this respect with other people.

I had no regrets about not swimming back to the Big Silver, but I did regret not finding the white Egyptian cotton tablecloth on Christmas Day the year before. In the end I'd had to use a white paper tablecloth. It didn't look that good, though I had suggested to my daughters that our table looked like the sort of French brasserie where the waiter writes our order on the corners of the paper cloth and then comes round later to add up the bill. They did not recall the sort of brasserie I had in mind and asked if I was going to charge our guests for Christmas lunch. This year the white Egyptian cotton cloth would be adorned with candles, red berries, holly and mistletoe. Their father would join us and I would invite the man who cried at the funeral and his new lover to join the table. And Celia, obviously, if she could fit me into her busy schedule. We decided to make cranberry as well as bread sauce, and swapped tips on how to make both. There was no way we could console each other for the undisclosed hurt that had contributed to sinking the boat, or for our lack of desire to swim back to it. Yet it was true that the societal mask of husband and wife, which we had worn for so long, had slipped, and we could see each other again. Perhaps what we saw was too human to bear. We stood up, put on our coats and kissed each other goodbye.

The night before, I had watched an interview on television with a middle-aged Mexican woman who worked as a dish-washer in a casino in Vegas. She had raised seven children, her son was serving in the Marines, she was speaking about fleeing to America when she was young. I was half listening and then I was completely listening. Her words opened a space, a wide-open space inside me. *'I crossed the border alone, I came feeling the black and bluish darkness, the howling of the coyotes, the sound of the plants.'*

When a woman has to find a new way of living and breaks from the societal story that has erased her name, she is expected to be viciously self-hating, crazed with suffering, tearful with remorse. These are the jewels reserved for her in the patriarchy's crown, always there for the taking. There are plenty of tears, but it is better to walk through the black and bluish darkness than reach for those worthless jewels.

Marguerite Duras suggested in a reverie that came to her from the calm of her final house, a home she had made to please herself, that 'writing comes like the wind'.

It's naked, it's made of ink, it's the thing written, and it passes like nothing else passes in life, nothing more, except life itself.

The writing you are reading now is made from the cost of living and it is made with digital ink.

Deborah Levy writes fiction, plays, and poetry. Her work has been staged by the Royal Shakespeare Company and widely broadcast on the BBC. The author of highly praised novels, including *Hot Milk* and *Swimming Home* (both Man Booker Prize finalists), *The Unloved*, and *Billy and Girl*, the story collection *Black Vodka*, and the memoir *Things I Don't Want to Know*, she lives in London. Levy is a fellow of the Royal Society of Literature.